POISE

FACING CANCER WITH GRACE AND
RESILIENCE

GAIL BOENNING

Editor: Noosha Ravaghi

Illustrator: Gail Boenning

Cover Design: Nathaniel Dasco

For Henrietta
whose leap made awareness, acceptance,
and action possible. May we continue our field
trips for many years to come.
Woof!

FOREWORD

Gail's cancer diagnosis was a moment of truth. She could have chosen to give in to fear and despair, but instead, she chose to approach her diagnosis with an open hand, eager for a dance partner. She found inspiration and resilience in the ordinary moments of her life, and she used her writing to connect with others and share her story.

I first met Gail through a small group of eclectic thinkers who met weekly to share and explore our creativity. When Gail was diagnosed with cancer, she continued to meet with us every Wednesday. Even on her hardest days, she brought joy and inspiration to our group.

I remember one Wednesday when Gail was feeling particularly down. She had just finished a round of treatment, and she was feeling tired and sick. But when she arrived at our meeting, she still had that twinkle in her eye — that twinkle I've come to recognize as Gail's spirit of creative connections. She told us about a bird and a flower that she encountered on her morning walk with her trusty dog Henny in a light rain. It was incredible to see Gail transform her rough day into a connection to a bird

singing in spite of the rain and connect to the flower that bene-
fits from that rain.

    Gail's series of vignettes have inspired me to open myself up
to the unexpected beauty of everyday moments. It has also
inspired me to share my own joy with others. I have started to
pay more attention to the small things in life, and I have found
that there is always something to be grateful for. I have also
started to share my own stories with others, to lean into my
creativity, and I have found that it is a great way to connect with
people and make a difference in the world.

    Gail's new writing on her journey with cancer is a delightful
and unpredictable inspiration. It is a reminder that even in the
midst of difficulty, there is always hope and beauty to be found.
I highly recommend her book, *Poise: Facing Cancer with Grace
and Resilience.*

1

OPEN

Open for business.
Open to let fresh air in.
Open to let the dog out.
Open to new possibilities.

Open to hear.
Open to reflect on the past and lessons learned.
Open to experience.
Open to uncertainty.
Open to change.
Open to see.
Open to acceptance.
Open to new ideas.
Open to growth.
Open to touch.
Open to putting fear in its place.
Open heart.
Open mind.
Open soul.
Simply open.

*O*n January 1, 2017, I made a declaration — the poem above — to the universe. At the time, I had no idea God would hear me, intensifying my path so that I could one day realize my full potential. The road has not been straight, flat, or smooth.

What I continue to adventure through on this third rock from the sun is challenge and struggle.

I *choose* to focus on the collateral beauty that holds hands with my pain.

I believe *this* is the meaning of *life*.

Through us, our higher power finds joy in living.

Our travels are not easy because
God, through us, wants to feel how big our brave *is.*

If you really want to find out what love is, don't be afraid — of anything.

~ J. Krishnamurti

2

CRAZY DOG

$\mathcal{O}$nce upon a brisk November's eve, I pull snow pants over my blue jeans, tie my boot laces, attach Henrietta's leash to her collar's metal ring, and set off through our garage into a starry night. Four paws prance and dance with enthusiasm as we descend the hill that slopes from our house toward the cul-de-sac. Near the bottom of the S-turn, where our drive flattens out, Henrietta grasps the leash between her canines and shakes her head. She jumps and lunges, hopeful I'll join her roughhousing game.

"Knock it off, Crazy Dog!" I shake the lead's handle, encouraging play. (I can only imagine our puppy-kindergarten instructor's dismay at my mixed signals.) Spurred on, Henrietta springs at me and her shoulder makes bone-to-bone contact with my chest.

"Yeowch!" I stop to catch my breath and to fondle my breast through multiple layers of purple parka, fleece zip-up, and turtleneck sweater. Tears prick my eyes. "That hurt, Henny!"

After a few moments of self-soothing, we walk on.

We do not cross paths with a human, car, whitetail, coyote, or cottontail under the stars. The whole neighborhood is quiet. Holiday lights twinkle from bare branches and peaked rooftops as in my mind I take full responsibility for the inciting shake that caused our crash.

Later, snug in my bed, as I press and poke at my newly tender flesh, I unsheath a quote that I sharpen and polish like a samurai to send negative thinking back to whence it came.

All shall be well, and all shall be well, and all manner of thing shall be well.

~ Julian of Norwich

3

TWO THINGS

wo things, Gail Lynn...
There are two things you NEVER want in your life!
Do you hear me?
Do NOT allow either of these to happen.
Understood?
First...
Debt
Never charge something that you cannot pay for at the same moment you put it on the plastic!

Do not carry debt for ANYTHING except a home... and maybe a vehicle.

Second...

Cancer

Do not allow any of your cells to go rogue and metastatic. Malignant is a word you must expunge from your vocabulary. If you ever get cancer, it will grab and mangle you like a Volkswagen Bug lifted, carried, and tossed in a tornado. You will suffer. Everyone who loves you will suffer. Most likely, you will wither, shrink, and die in a sterile room amid the chirps and beeps of machines.

Hmmm... Is it possible to write stories other than the ones we've been handed?

You never know what you can do until you try, and very few try unless they have to.

~ C.S. Lewis

BIG SCARY #1

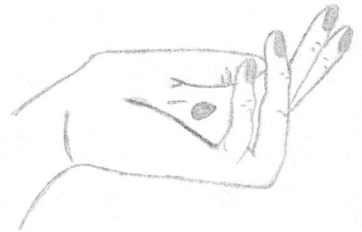

*I*f I pause and reflect, do I have any undercurrents of unease flowing inside me? Remnants of my childhood?

For much of my life I've carried two big scary *what-ifs.* The first relates to money, which I suspect is nearly universal.

What happens if I go broke?

What if I can't pay my bills?

What if I end up homeless?

What if I can't buy food?

What if...?

My father, who survived the great depression, taught me

how to live a life of financial security and stability. I learned to be fastidious about a balanced checkbook and to pay every bill on time. The only debt I allow is *reasonable* — a home loan, a car loan, credit card purchases that can be paid off when the statement arrives by mail.

Responsible and *safe*...

At least to the extent that one can prepare for the unknown...

What I sometimes wonder though is: *Can one play life too safely?*

How many adventures have I turned down because of financial fear?

And is it possible that a little risk carries pounds of possibility?

———

A father prepares to leave on a summer journey and entrusts his three children with various *seeds*.

The child who is given five seeds sets to work immediately. She plants and tends a plot that produces an abundance of fruit.

The child who receives two seeds plants one in the open field and the other among the thistle. He splits his risk with an awareness that the seed planted in the open is vulnerable to hungry rabbits, whereas the thistle-sheltered seed has to compete for water and light. One seed fails, but the other fills the boy's bushel basket to its brim.

The third child receives only one seed. Overcome with indecision, she tucks the pip into her pocket for safe keeping. There, it stands no chance at all.

When the father returns, he takes great joy in the efforts of two of his children. With the third child, he finds an opportunity to teach. "Child," he asks, "if you do not believe and invest in yourself, why should anybody else?"

What is the cost of playing too safe?

Fear of life closes off more opportunities for us than fear of death ever does.

~ Agnes Moorehead

BIG SCARY #2

$\mathcal{S}$ ometime between my eighth and ninth birthdays, my mom vomited blood. Anything I tell you about what happened between that momentous puke and her death, a year and a half later, would be about as accurate as a report from a blind and deaf pedestrian recounting the events of a hit and run two blocks away. In an attempt to make sense of what was happening around me, my ten-year-old brain clung to certain events, took a few snapshots, and swallowed the world's stories like cold medicine delivered on a silver spoon. Intended to heal, the syrup left me jaded. I carried the aftertaste as I grew into an adult.

> *My mother's death from lung cancer at the age of*
>   *thirty-eight taught me that...*
> *a motherless daughter is a victim*
> *cancer's treatment is worse than the disease*
> *having cancer is a burden to everyone who loves you*
>
> *So... I decided that:*
> *I would never be a victim — of anything*
> *cancer was not invited to my house,*
> *but if it showed up as a squatter,*
> *I'd ignore the invader and keep it a secret.*

My scars needed softening. For much of my life, I believed that if cancer took up residence in my frame, I'd live out the rest of my days as best as I could while tossing a blanket over the elephant.

Thank God I have given myself permission to change my mind!

Seriously, fifty years of cancer treatment advancements is something to trumpet about.

Some things are best mended by a break.
    ~ Edith Wharton

6

SPACIOUS

I lie on my back. My right arm rests on a pillow above my head. A heated blanket covers my ribs, belly, and legs. Because I said yes, a cotton ball saturated with lavender essential oil is taped to the left shoulder of my robe.

"If I didn't know better," I joke, "I could pretend I'm enjoying a day at the spa."

"We know how stressful a biopsy can be and do our best to make you comfortable."

Ever an optimist, I'm still convincing myself this is all for naught, a monetary transaction between a clinic and an insurance company. I surely don't have cancer. Of course, I don't say this out loud... because *what if I'm wrong?*

I stare at the ceiling. A genius somewhere acted on a brilliant idea, creating outer space mere feet above my head. I tell myself that if I stand on the exam table (safer than the stools with wheels) I can touch the moon, catch a shooting star, sparkle like a heavenly body...

Despite many minutes of rolling her ultrasound wand around and inside my armpit, my carer cannot locate what she must find. A suspicious lymph node, documented only two days earlier at my mammogram, plays a relentless game of hide and seek. I sense a fuzzy monster running through her mind. Her frustration is felt, yet I am aware that it's self-directed.

"Anything I can do to help?"

"No, thank you. I can usually find the trickiest of nodes," she sighs. "I'm going to have to ask for the doctor's help. Your arm has been raised for a long time. Would you like to bring it down for a rest?"

"No, no. I'm fine." I want to scold my body for thwarting her efforts. She's been kind, gentle, and warm with her words, manner, and touch.

She makes a call. Within moments, the radiologist floats into our starlit scene.

———————

False bravado?

   Self-defense?

   Trauma-induced memory loss?

   Or, simply being me — announcing my rebel kindness?

   I act as if I'm enjoying a wilderness overnight with new friends.

I peer into the night sky and get curious. I don't ask questions about the procedure or the extraction of cancerous cells — nope, I get curious about the ladies taking care of me. Over the next thirty minutes, while they do their jobs with tender care, I ask questions. I learn about their families, what books they are reading, and how they came to their professions. By the time the gel is toweled from my armpit and I'm sitting upright, I feel as if I have two new friends. The reality is I'll likely never see them again.

I waltz to another room for one more post-procedure dance with a mammography machine before heading home. The initial results will be available in about twenty-four hours. I should receive a call from the radiologist on duty tomorrow afternoon.

And even though nothing is normal, I drive home, walk Henrietta, and act as if everything is exactly as it should be.

Worry is a waste of imagination.
~ Walt Disney

7

THE MACHINE

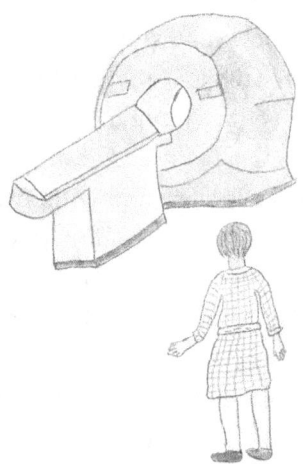

he Saturday and Sunday sandwiched between Friday's diagnosis and Monday morning's breast MRI lie as low as a bucket down a well. I take up residence in a corner of my newly painted and polished home studio. I feel the sting of a sucker-punch to my gut and am either unwilling or unable to find any positive possibilities in my new reality. My upcycled table from the charity shop sits dormant, holding brushes, markers, and pencils in tidy jars and containers.

For hours at a time, a worn burgundy wing chair holds me, along with a fistful or more of shed Labrador hair. I telephone my father, brother, and sister to break the news. Another among us has been caught by C. I read and stream entertainment on my phone. I resist all urges to surf and investigate the unknown future I am walking toward. I'm challenged to wrap my head around my new reality. For four decades I declared cancer an unwelcome guest. Diseases care little about manners.

On Monday morning I shower, shave armpits and legs, and dress in winter layers — sans jewelry. *Metal messes with the magnets...* I check in at the lobby kiosk and share my name with an imaging receptionist. I'm taken directly to a conjoined changing and waiting room, where I take off all my layers, except underwear and socks, and stuff them into a lock-by-code cubby. Unlike the undersized locker, the robe I slip into is large enough to hold three of me. I cinch, blouse, and adjust the waffle-weave before taking a tan tweed seat.

I am alone. The space is stark and without reading materials. Even though the pandemic is winding down, maybe a fear of shared touchables lingers? I contemplate an oak-framed print of daisies bending in the wind, while worrying the waist tie of my robe with my fingers.

I work on my self-talk. *It'll be fine. You're not claustrophobic. You are not sensitive to noise. You'll breathe... slow and deep.*

A technician dressed in scrubs and soft shoes comes to retrieve me. She takes me to a room where I sit in a leather recliner. I hike up the robe's sleeves and rest my arms on tray tables so that she can have a look at the superhighways transporting my blood.

"Arm preference?"

"Nope."

She chooses my left elbow pit because it's my non-dominant arm. She slides a needle into my vein, allowing dye to mix and mingle with my blood.

Check!

I rise and follow her through a second door. We enter a dark space resembling a NASA control room. Another tech stands in front of a long desk of computery contraptions. The third doorless doorway brings me face to face with the tube.

I untie my robe and lie face down on the table. I focus on my breath and listen to directions delivered through speakers.

"Please keep your breathing shallow," instructs one of my caregivers. "The machine is very sensitive to movement. We want to get you through this procedure as quickly as possible, without retakes."

As a rule follower extraordinaire, I slam dunk my deep breathing plan into the trash receptacle by the door. With mindfully shallow breaths, I make it through the forty-minute procedure without a hitch and am escorted back to the changing room. I'm delighted to remember the secret code I programmed into cubby number seven. I collect my layers, dress, and wait with the daisies to meet my nurse navigator.

Gem, an unexpected lifeline, arrives within minutes. She's dressed like springtime in a flowered blouse. She leads me down a maze of quiet hallways to a private room. There she shares my current pathology results that are still not definitive as to my cancer type. HER2 or Triple Negative remains an unsolved mystery. Together we explore a thick white binder bearing a red title: Cancer Care Guide. Gem shares the schedule of appointments she's secured on my behalf. My calendar squares for the next two weeks are penciled with medical appointments. Generally not one who likes to be touched, I find comfort in Gem's hand on my bicep as she walks me to the sliding glass doors.

Free from the clinic, I cross the parking lot, climb into my truck, and sob. Like the robe, my life no longer fits.

I'm unsure of what I fear more, cancer... or a medical machine that has yet to earn my trust.

———————

Experience is a hard teacher because she gives the test first, the lesson afterward.
~ Vernon Law

8

THE BAG

There are times when we need room
      to grow into better versions of ourselves.
Sometimes we need more space than others.

This
is one of those times
when
I
need

Grand Canyon-like
roominess.

Flowers in shades of fuchsia, tangerine, violet, and teal announce themselves on a heavy-weight, black fabric background. "Volunteers sew and donate the carry bags." Gem explains as she pulls a matching mini pillow from the satchel, then slides the Cancer Care binder into its roomy interior. "The pillow is for after your port surgery — a comfort between your chest and the seat belt."

Along with a slew of ruckus making, fear- and anger-fueled thoughts, one stands out and grumbles *Great. Just one more thing I don't want.*

I sling bright-and-cheery over my shoulder and tote it to my truck. Alone, I allow myself to fall apart before reassembling what's necessary to shift myself back into drive.

At home, I shrug the satchel's straps onto the back of a kitchen chair, willfully ignoring its contents. Eyes wide open, I choose to take information and moments as they come. At this time, without clear pathology results, the binder is only a game of *if this, then that.* I refuse to play.

When my husband gets home from work, he motions at the chair and asks, "What's that?"

"That..." I reply, "is ugly. A gift... made by a volunteer. Doesn't it scream CANCER PATIENT? I am NEVER going to use it." I pull out the pillow and hold it up. "To protect me from my seat belt — after port surgery."

Embarrassed.

I feel shame over my petulance and ingratitude.

The feeling is neither right nor wrong.

What matters is my awareness... and the choices I make going forward.

Over the next two weeks, I shuffle the bag and its contents from the kitchen table to the family room recliner to the table in my studio. After a diagnosis of Triple Negative cells is confirmed, I explore the contents of the white binder, paying attention to what's relevant to my treatment protocol. I'm still not a fan of the satchel as a fashion accessory, but I'm becoming used to its presence in my life. I tuck the coordinating pillow into our truck's console so that I'll have it come port surgery day.

On the third of March, the day of my first chemotherapy infusion, I load *bright and cheery* to its brim. Yes, it holds the binder — along with sketch paper, drawing and colored pencils, books to read for pleasure, a sliced apple, almonds, yogurt, a plastic spoon, and a water bottle. I tell myself that if it screams CANCER PATIENT, that's just fine. I AM a cancer patient... at a cancer center... receiving cancer treatment.

Somehow over the space of two weeks, I am able to cast aside fear and anger to replace them with gratitude and love. I find myself wishing I could hold the hands of the volunteer who crafted my floral satchel. I wish I could look into their eyes and tell them how much the bag means to me, how awed I am that they gave, expecting nothing in return.

Looking back, I am able to hold ungrateful Gail with compassion.

Often...
we
simply
need

time
and
space

to
learn
and
grow.

Between stimulus and response there is a space. In that space is our power to choose our response. In our response lies our growth and our freedom.

~ Viktor Frankl

PINCHED FOR GROWTH

"The bone scan is clear. I do see a crack in your tailbone — and a healed rib?"

"The rib happened years ago. And the tailbone... I slipped and fell on ice a few days before my mammogram. It still hurts, but nothing like it did during the first week after my slip." I shrug and stand up. "I can walk my dog at a normal pace again."

Today's waffle-weave robe has a bluish tint. I wonder if

that's intentional or if there was some kind of an oops at the laundry.

"I'll walk you back to the changing area."

As I bundle myself into my sweatshirt, blue jeans, and boots, I remember the story my blogging friend Manu shared with me in January.

Ahhh! January 2022...
the month before February...
the month before the everyday nips and tweaks of
    my life turned into
welt raising pinches.

Pinch for Growth
Manu Satsangi's Allegory

This is [a c]urry leaf plant.
This is a staple plant for Indian cooking.
It is kept indoors these days to escape the freezing.
This curry leaf plant is 5 years old
and it never really had much growth
until (...) last summer.
This summer my mother told me,

just pinch the top and then the plant will branch out.
If it does not branch out, just continue to pinch.
And it worked.
It started branching out and grew big too.
Humans also can evolve and grow with pinching!

In the first month of what would grow into a pivotal year, I clicked, opened, and read Manu's parable. With the arrogance of one who understands too quickly, I missed the message inside the message. Instead, I thought about my prowess at pinching lanky pansies and petunias on humid August days.

Yup! Okay! I got it!

I deleted the story from my inbox, but not from my memory.

In February, pinches piled, squeezing one big *scary* on top of another over the course of a few weeks.

slip, crack — falling and cracking my tailbone

poke, slap — biopsy revealing cancer

truck, rack — five thousand dollar transmission replacement

dog, zap — Hen's allergic reaction: eyes swell to golf-ball size, demanding veterinary care

From the depths of memory, I'm thrown a life preserver.

Humans also can evolve and grow with pinching!

Thanks, Manu.

Life only demands from you the strength you possess. Only one feat is possible — not to have run away.

~ Dag Hammarskjold

BOUNDARIES

*a*s if below a cloud-dotted sky, my mood shifts between light and shade.

Faith and hope that cancer came to increase the brightness of my flame, rather than to snuff me out, flits and flutters with fear and doubt.

The puny human that I am recognizes that this is the dance of life.

Will you choose fear or faith?

And though you be but little, are you aware that your choices radiate and create far beyond what you can see?

My vision is so limited that I choose to lean on a power far greater than my own.

I choose faith.

That said, fear and frustration do not disappear. Instead, *shade* emotions offer a trunk to push against, so that I can continue my climb toward the canopy.

One of the ways this plays out is through my relationships. As I interact with friends and family, I observe myself and the people I am talking to. The people-pleaser deep within me feels a pinch to moderate, facilitate, and placate the feelings of others. I sense their helplessness and desires to assist. I want to make space for their stories, advice, and offers of food, rides, and gifts, but the sting of my diagnosis waggles its bee butt.

> *You have cancer... and believe it or not... welts come with benefits.*
> *Perhaps it's time for you to expand your boundary-setting abilities?*
> *Time to practice saying no...*
> *Who's gonna hold that against you?*

LOVE LETTERS TO MY SISTER start appearing daily in my email inbox.

In the ten years between my sister's mastectomy and my diagnosis, our connection has been like a lightning bug with faulty wiring — illuminating briefly — with long dark intervals between flashes. I believe she's writing from a place of love and concern, but my red, swollen lenses see dirt instead of flowers.

These letters are uninvited and filled with advice — too much, too fast. Instead of cultivating the feelings of love I suspect she intends, I feel suffocated and frustrated. I don't want some-

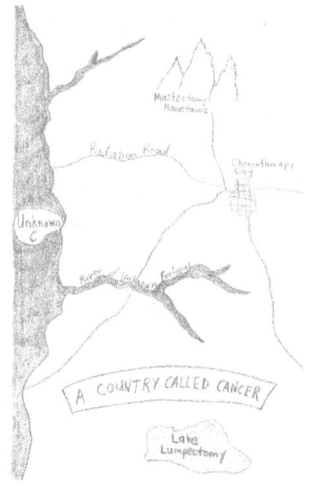

body else's map to a place I've never been. Odd as it might sound, I want to do cancer my way.

At this point, I still don't know what type of cancer I have, and until the results come in, I don't know what my treatment plan will include. Surgery? Radiation? Chemotherapy?

After reading her third dispatch, I pause, breathe, and reflect. Earlier that morning, when my dog whimpered at her empty water bowl, I scratched her ear and said, "I love that you tell me exactly what you need and want."

You can't be mad at people for sucking the nectar out of you if you keep giving them the straw.

When I hit the reply arrow, I'm honest and kind while at the same time setting a clear boundary.

I'm learning quickly that others sometimes feel helpless and/or feel like they need to step in with stories, advice, and offers of assistance.

Several have asked me what I want... how I want to be treated. This is the most helpful response I have received as it empowers me to take responsibility for my own feelings and engagement going forward. Also, these people trust me to reach out if I want/need something. Excessive attention makes me feel smothered. We are all different.

Please respect my request to be treated as you would have treated me a week ago... unless I ask for something different.

Although I'm aware you are acting with loving intent, daily emails are not something that I want.

Cancer has become a part of my life, but it is not my identity. I am neither a victim nor a warrior... I am a student of life and intend to live my own questions through this experience.

The courage it takes for me to set this boundary is rewarded. If my sister feels hurt or angry, she does not toss those feelings back at me. This speaks to her love and respect. I'm grateful. The daily letters stop. I believe our relationship is stronger because I dared to be brave.

Thank you, Cancer, for making space for me to practice setting boundaries.

I will keep going and growing — stronger because I have learned.

You teach people how to treat you by what you allow, what you stop, and what you reinforce.

~ Tony Gaskins

11

DRAGON

*I*t's late afternoon.

With a slight bend in my knees, I stand on kitchen tiles. I plant my socked and slippered feet hips' distance apart. As my shoulder blades relax down my back, my elbows point at the floor while my thumbs point toward each other.

I am a dragon... standing between heaven and earth.

The timer on my phone ticks off two long minutes with determination. *Can you stretch your fire-breathing power grab to three, four, or five minutes?*

Effort extended, I text Kate to let her know I've taken action.

God bless them; people want to help.

I want to help.

And, I want to be grateful... and to please the people who try to help me.

Kate and I met online as part of an entrepreneurial group. Every week she'd draw a card from her deck and read its Eastern-philosophy wisdom out loud. The group always marveled at how relevant the magical draw was to whatever we were discussing. As a believer in synchronicity and messages from the universe, I dug it.

My business is a mash-up of curiosity, creativity, and connection. Kate's business centers on Chinese medicine. So when I shared my breast cancer diagnosis with the group and Kate sent me a private message, asking if I'd like to meet one-to-one, *yes* was as automatic as my truck's transmission.

This morning, sitting in front of my computer screen, waiting for our video chat to begin, I fiddled with my plant-a-pencil that has a tiny plastic green cap of seeds where an eraser would normally sit. Basil. I'd had the pencil for years and never planted it. I wondered if seeds expire when not given an opportunity to grow.

Kate appeared on screen. For about an hour I listened as she explained various tenets of Chinese medicine.

She talked about her teacher, Master Lu.

I sketched a dragon.

She offered a list of ten balancing properties.

I wrote them down... and drew fire.

We smiled and nodded at each other.

"Yup... a cancer diagnosis sucks, but you might be able to fix yourself if only you correct your imbalances."

Wait, what?

Despite years of yoga and a belief that an East-meets-West approach to disease makes good sense, I bubbled with resentment. I tried to follow Walt Whitman's advice to be curious and not judgemental, but there was a fire kindling in my depths.

Is she saying I gave myself cancer?

Is she implying, through her philosophy, that having cancer is my fault?

Is she, whose table overflows with books and mess, who knows nothing about my life — how hard I have been working to balance myself and my thinking — suggesting I'm to blame?

Feeling it would be impolite to challenge, I kept these questions locked inside of my head. I smiled and nodded. And after we hung up, I felt angry, confused, and defeated.

It's late afternoon...

While prepping dinner, I watch Master Lu execute the dragon's pose between heaven and earth.

With a slight bend in my knees, I stand on kitchen tiles. I plant my socked and slippered feet hips' distance apart. As my shoulder blades relax down my back, my elbows point at the floor while my thumbs point toward each other.

I am a dragon, standing between heaven and earth.

I feel... ridiculous.

With true appreciation for her time, I text Kate to let her know I've taken action, but in my heart I've decided: Like it or not, my path is going to be paved with the big guns of chemotherapy, surgery, and radiation. Bring on the oncologist! I might be a dragon... but I'm also a dragon slayer and this battle is going to require the assistance of big pharma.

> *Can you hear me, God?*
> *It's Gail.*
> *What is this all supposed to be teaching me?*

It simply isn't an adventure worth telling if there aren't any dragons.

~ J.R.R. Tolkien

12

BLURRY

*T*he weather outside was — *Okay, I don't remember the day's weather.* My internal weather was (and is) a bit shrouded in mist — fuzzing the details from that first meeting with my oncologist.

Nurse Winona collected me from the waiting room and then collected my vitals with her tools — scale, thermometer, blood pressure cuff, and a litany of questions that, in the coming months, I would learn to anticipate and answer before they were asked.

At some point, I changed into a robe and the doctor completed a physical exam of my marauding mass. I recall telling him that since being biopsied, the lump seemed angry. "Is that possible, or is it an illusion of my mind?"

At our first meet-and-greet, Doctor S shared a lot of information with me and my spouse. At no point did I feel him rushing or hurrying us along. Like my nurse navigator and my surgeon, he began with an explanation of the flavor and severity of the rogue cells in my breast.

Breast cancer is classified in four ways — estrogen fueled, progesterone fueled, HER2, and Triple Negative. The lab's investigation of my tissue determined I was facing Triple Negative, which simply means that the other three breast cancer diagnoses did not fit. Triple Negative tends to have an aggressive nature and is therefore treated with the heaviest hand.

The measurements showed that in the nineteen months between mammograms, I'd grown a little 4.2 x 3.4 x 1 centimeter monster. Huh. Based on size and lack of lymph node involvement, I walked the staging border between a two and a three.

"What difference does the staging number make?"

My hazy memory recalls the answer having something to do with insurance approvals and clinical trial possibilities. When all was said and done, I think I was staged at a two — *which should have made me happy?*

Doctor S drew a map outlining my treatment on a 4 x 6 slip of white paper. The plan contained many-lettered pharmaceutical names, timeframes, arrows, and surgery. He covered every possible side-effect from hair loss to neuropathy, mouth sores and fatigue to lost fingernails and wonky blood counts.

When it was my turn to ask questions, I couldn't not ask the question I carried for much of my life.

"What happens if I do nothing?"

"The cancer will continue to grow and spread. You will likely die a slow and painful death."

"Thank you," I replied. "Of course I will be going ahead with treatment, but I had to ask."

The yellow carbon copy of the Consent for Chemotherapy and/or Biotherapy Treatment for Cancer that I signed that day became a beacon of hope. Where it said *Goals of Therapy*, Doctor S wrote: *CURE*.

Remembering my conversation with a practitioner of Eastern medicine and wondering what the West might have to say about my culpability in this matter, I asked, "What causes triple-negative breast cancer?"

I was certain I was with the right doctor when he replied, "Dumb luck."

Because of COVID-19 masking protocols, it would be a month or more before I learned that Dr. S had a beard and a warm smile. Several weeks after our first visit, the doctor who never once made me feel rushed, shared that it was his son's birthday. He told me about his family's plans to celebrate and then showed me a couple of family photos stored on his cell phone.

What I DO remember clearly from our first meeting is that Doctor S was kind, that I trusted him to guide me through whatever would come next, and that we shared a love of ice cream.

What more could I have asked for?

Without ice cream, there would be darkness and chaos.
~ Don Kardong

13

GROWING PAINS

*M*y mind motors in multiple directions —
berating, bolstering, bending with each erratic
thought.

Was it my fault?
Was it her fault?
The communication was unclear.

I should have called to verify.

She should have said there was a procedural time change in her voicemail message...

I have just been diagnosed with breast cancer... my liver enzymes are too high... I'm here for a CT scan to see if there's cancer in my liver and a bone scan for good measure... and... SHE HAS THE AUDACITY TO SCOLD ME?

A young man with short dark hair pulls me from my thoughts. "Gail? Gail Bone-ing?"

Can't fault anyone for mispronouncing my last name. Why the ancestors didn't drop the "o" if they wanted to be called Ben-ing is an excellent question. I grab my two plastic water bottles containing the fluid I need to drink and follow my leader.

Outside of the oncologist, this is my first male caregiver. I find that interesting, but in my flustered state, curiosity is relegated to the back seat. If I had my wits about me, I would ask many questions. The monkeys in my mind gobble up my presence and wits as if they were peanuts and popcorn.

He verifies my name and birthdate before scanning my bracelet and tying an elastic band around my bicep. I look away while the needle punctures my vein.

"Thank you. I hardly felt a thing."

"It doesn't have to hurt." The crinkles around his eyes tell me his smile is warm, even though his mask keeps it hidden from me.

"I'm a little worried about the woman I've upset at the desk."

"Don't be," he replies without elaboration. My monkeys whip up a story about her. *She's likely a bitter, crotchety hag... as insensitive with her coworkers as she is with the patients. I'll bet nobody likes her.*

The tech of few-but-impactful words escorts me back to the waiting room, where in my absence, the receptionist — whom I thought of as my jousting partner — has placed calls and asked questions of those who make decisions about errant eaters. *Yes... even though I ate oatmeal within the forbidden time frame, testing will proceed as originally scheduled.* Peace is restored.

As I sip my thirty-two ounces of pre-procedure H_2O, I listen to my monkey's chatter. Even though all is now well, I can hear shame sloshing around with my fluids. My blunder or not, I feel like a naughty child. I turn my attention to the black-haired receptionist to whom I'd hastily assigned an unsavory persona. She felt that yesterday's phone message was clear — that she'd done her due diligence. *Was her bluster toward me fueled by fluster, too?*

Taking time to explore my feelings opens up space for inner and outer compassion to flow. With my ruffled feathers settled, I turn my attention to the book I brought to calm my mind's fiddle-faddle. Reaching through time, via words printed on a page, Father Anthony De Mello reminds me that awareness makes all the difference in a life.

Do change and growth hurt? Or does our pain grow out of resistance to them?

You don't always get to choose the load, but you can choose how to carry it.

~ James Clear

I-TEAM

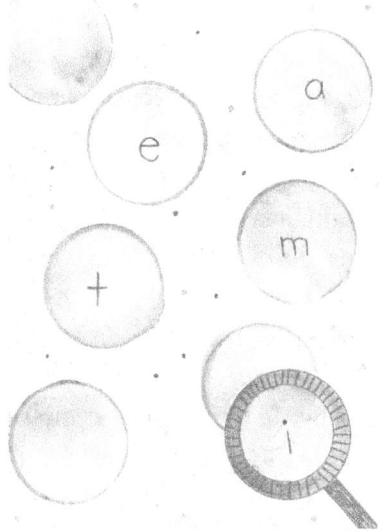

$\mathcal{P}$ ancreatic cancer caught him.

   Before that happened, though, he changed the world.

 Personal computers, smartphones, and computer-animated films ride his creative wake.

I wonder what the mastermind behind the iPod, iPhone, and iPad thought about the cliché: *There's no "i" in team.*

An online search tells me that the (i) stands for internet, as well as imagination and individuality which are integral values of the big Apple vision.

I have great respect for Steve Jobs as an innovator, leader, and individual contributor to Team Humanity.

In a 2005 commencement address, he looked back at his life and the priceless learning he stumbled into by following his curiosity and intuition. He concluded, "You can't connect the dots looking forward. You can only connect them looking backwards."

Do you ever look back at your dots to extract your priceless learnings?

When I reflect and focus my lens for optimum viewing, I see dots — dots that prepared me to face cancer and its treatment with a courageous heart. I'm ready to rewrite the cancer script that lives in my head. A smile in my soul welcomes the challenge of rolling up my sleeves and doing my best, come what may.

On Monday mornings when surgical, medical, and radiation oncology caregivers meet to discuss my case, along with many others, I will be there in spirit. At my clinic visits, I will radiate warmth and kindness of such magnitude that everyone on my care team will be pulling for me to win.

I will be the "I" in TEAM, taking my responsibility as an individual contributor to the highest heights.

Win or lose, I'm gonna play my heart out... because I'm worth it.

The idea is not to live forever, but to create something that will.

~ Andy Warhol

15

LIBRARY REINFORCEMENTS

$\mathcal{I}$'ve heard rumblings that some people don't like libraries — book treasuries regarded as an unnecessary community expense. *Who wants to touch pages smeared with mysterious smudges? Everything's available online these days, isn't it? All of those germs!*

Oh well, everyone is entitled to their opinion.

For me, a library is a vibrant sanctuary. Is there any other space where you can hold art collections in your hands, travel from Antarctica to Zimbabwe, surf the waves of time, sit quietly in reverie, or debate the merits of town renovation in a private room? Let's not forget the romantic affairs that are available mere feet from Dr. Seuss and Winnie the Pooh.

In many of my precious memories, I sit surrounded by book-lined shelves and a pull-drawer cabinet filled with Dewey Decimal System cards.

I grew up in the 70s, singing along to songs with titles like *I Will Survive, I Think I Love You, We've Only Just Begun,* and *Shake Your Booty.* On warm summer days, my neighborhood friends and I commandeered the library steps with a transistor radio. Our undeveloped voices sang along as we danced and practiced cartwheels on the sidewalk. No one cared — just kids being kids.

Outside of the Cream City brick building, we were loud.

Inside, we respected the rule of hushed reverence, well... mostly.

How many hours did I spend trying to paraphrase Encyclopedia Britannica's articles for school reports? How many times did I watch Olivia Newton-John and John Travolta sing, dance, and act out a story of young love as old as time on a new invention called a VHS player? Is that little girl me, reading a story about *Stone Soup*... feelings of accomplishment encircling my folding chair as my peers sit cross-legged on carpet squares?

Years later...

I shared my love for the library with a child of my own. In another small town, on a wall-to-wall, small-loop Berber rug, we listened to children's librarian Miss Jane read about lions, tigers, and bears. We ventured through the holidays with characters like the Berenstain Bears and a lime green frog named Froggy. *Thomas the Train, The Very Hungry Caterpillar,* and *The Magic Tree House* series taught us both about courage, transformation, and possibility. Sometimes, we even checked out cassette tapes that we then blasted through our sedan speakers on summer days. *Freight train, freight train...*

Fast forward to middle age...

I called my local Literacy Council with an aspiration to tutor non-native English speakers in reading, but the universe had a different plan. I was paired with Donna, a woman seven or eight years my senior, with whom I shared many demographic labels — white, American, Midwestern, female, etcetera. There are also a number of glaring differences — including education level and economic stability. As best I could discern, Donna was dyslexic or had another form of learning disability. She read at a second- or third-grade level. Together we marveled at how she graduated high school. Now in her early fifties, she continued to be blessed with burning curiosity and a desire to learn. We met weekly, ditching the Literacy Council's boring curriculum, to read *Charlotte's Web*, *Little House on the Prairie*, *Ramona the Pest*, and *Tales of a Fourth Grade Nothing*. Our crowning moment arrived when Donna sat in Miss Jane's folding chair to read a book about a bunny-challenged gardener aloud to a group of toddlers and their mothers.

Surrounded by computers, periodicals, and people from all walks of life, Donna and I built a rest-of-our-lives friendship — in large part, thanks to a library.

Within weeks of my cancer diagnosis...

A group of feisty librarians offer me inspiration.

A message from the Ukraine Library Association circulates

social media near the time of my first chemotherapy infusion. Ukraine is under attack from Russia and the librarians' forthcoming conference is canceled. They announce: "We will reschedule just as soon as we have finished vanquishing our invaders."

If the Ukrainian librarians can keep going with humor and a fighting spirit, so can I.

Libraries always remind me that there are good things in this world.

~ Lauren Ward

16

BRAVE

*I*f you put your mind to it, becoming a professional happens in a snap.

A
professional
shows up
wearing her
can-do attitude
game face
smile at the ready

Kind words
and love
ooze
from her pockets

Several weeks in, with shock dispersed into my morning cup, acceptance is the cream that tempers my new normal. I dress for success, aware that once I arrive at my new *job* I'll be slipping into a waffle-weave, waist-belted uniform. My face is powdered. My lips are tinted. And, as instructed, all jewelry rests at home in its box.

The surface I lie upon is hard. In contrast, the lighted ceiling tiles above soften my day's business with pink cherry blossoms. A blanket, fresh from the warmer, covers me. I've quickly learned to *always* accept the heated comfort when offered.

This machine talks.

Breathe in.

Hold.

Breathe out.

Hold.

Beeeep!

Imaging complete, I'm asked to sit up and gather my bearings before standing.

Maggie, my machine tech, offers a verbal high-five. "You did great in there. One and done."

Like most humans, I love a good ego scratch.

"I'm trying to be the best patient I can be."

Maggie leans close and whispers, "I shouldn't say this, but... you'll get better care because of that."

Huh...

I unlock my cubby, retrieve my street clothes, and slide shut the frosted glass door of my changing room. As I drop the robe and get dressed, I think about the word *should*. It's subjective, and often out of step with reality — out of sync with what *is*.

I *shouldn't* have cancer, but I do.

I *should* be scared, but I'm not.

I *should* be sad, or anxious, or frustrated, or angry, but why?

What if, instead, I choose to be confident, creative, present, and joyful?

What happens when I choose to be the best patient I can be?

I'm going to find out... by walking the walk and talking the talk.

Whether or not Maggie *should* have suggested I'd get better care, she spoke a universal truth, and I love her for saying what she wanted to say.

———————

Life is an echo. What you send out, comes back. What you sow, you reap.

~ Zig Ziglar

17

LIFT ME

I always said I was like those round-bottomed circus dolls — you know, those dolls you could push down and they'd come back up? I've always been like that. I've always said, No matter what happens, if I get pushed down, I'm going to come right back up.

~ Doris Day

I tumble through thin air.
My heart catches
on branches of emotion.
My head catches
on mountains of information.
My body catches
on sensations shrouded in doubt.

Are the twinges of pain in my breast real or imagined?

I can compare the weeks following my biopsy and diagnosis to a day at the circus.

There's the danger of a man-eating lion.

Synchronization of appointments requires the precision of trapeze artists.

I'm gifted a ring master (nurse navigator) who keeps our show running on schedule.

There's a feeling of being shot from a cannon.

I'm tested and treated in a big top focused on comfort, engagement, and palatability.

Let's not forget the peanuts, popcorn, and cotton candy...

Friends, family, acquaintances — strangers, even! — give me gifts, both tangible and intangible.

Blankets, books, mugs, tea, headcoverings, puzzles, anti-nausea drops, gift cards, and so much more find their way into my hands.

Prayers, well-wishes, and kind words find their way into my heart.

Humorous signs, slogans, and t-shirt sayings amuse my mind.

In one of my earliest public love letters, sent after my diagnosis, I spill the beans and say:

As a private person, telling family and friends about my diagnosis has been... like trying to earn a college degree in a week.

Not only have I been observing myself and my emotions, I've been watching everyone else, too.

I have been empowered by some who have asked, "How would you like to be treated?"

I love this question because it shifts complete responsibility to me... and frees the asker. They do not have to operate on assumptions or show care in ways that I might or might not find helpful. I feel trusted... and in that trust I will feel comfortable asking for what I need.

You can help by... sharing funny and/or uplifting messages, video clips, and photos. Please help me to keep my thoughts in the light.

In response to every blog post I write over the course of a year, my friend Jack comments with a quip to tickle my funny bone.

Following are a few of my favorites:

- *A typo walks into a bra.*
- *Handle stress like a dog. If you can't eat it or play with it, pee on it and walk away.*
- *An optimist stays until midnight to see the New Year in. A pessimist stays up to make sure the old year leaves.*
- *I was addicted to The Hokey Pokey... but then I turned myself around.*
- *Time flies like an arrow; fruit flies like a banana.*
- *To the person who invented zero, thanks for nothing.*
- *To the person who stole my antidepressants: I hope you're happy now.*
- *I had a hen who could count her own eggs. She was a* mathemachicken.

- *Had a big mix up at the store today. Apparently when the woman said, "Strip down facing me," she was referring to my credit card.*

Jack tossed me something to smile at every single day for an entire year.

If that's not love, I don't know what is.

There is no exercise better for the heart than reaching down and lifting people up.

~ John Holmes

Junk Mail Can Be Our Friend
Written by Jack Herlocker

My wife, Deb, and I like to read the junk catalogs we get in the mail. We started years ago, to have something to keep our minds occupied while eating breakfast. The cute things (or strange things, or implausible things, or implausibly strange things) we share with each other. For years I've been posting some of the things we find on Medium, in a running series as part of my "Chats with Deb" posts.

Funny sayings on t-shirts and signs are favorites.

When Gail announced her cancer, I did not have any words of solace or comfort. I'm not good at that sort of thing. (I do decent hugs, but those lack a little something digitally.) But I did have a series of odd little jokes revolving around language and punctuation that I'd just run across, and since Gail is a words person...

So I posted one a day to her blog. And quickly realized, as

they were received well, that I would need a few more. Okay, time to raid the archives for old posts with quips stolen from our junk mail collection!

I created, and kept expanding, an internal document titled "Quips for Gail", and as I used each quip it got a checkmark so I knew what I'd used. I also raided Facebook and (oddly enough) the Q&A site Quora, which has a fair amount of humor on it. T-shirts, signs, buttons, the odd meme or a cute caption if it worked without the picture — all fair game.

Sometimes I picked something not actually humorous. But still appropriate.

- Necklace: "Fate whispers to the warrior, 'You cannot withstand the storm.' The warrior whispers back, 'I AM THE STORM.'"
- Bracelet: "I alone cannot change the world, but I can cast a stone across the waters to create many ripples"
- Sign: "Do not just slay your inner demons; dissect them and find out what they've been feeding on."

And when Gail got back the ultimate cancer results with the good news, I knew I was finished, mission accomplished. Big smile.

Not that I don't still have a few quips left for when I don't have any cogent comments on her blog post...

18

LIKE THE DAY YOU WERE BORN

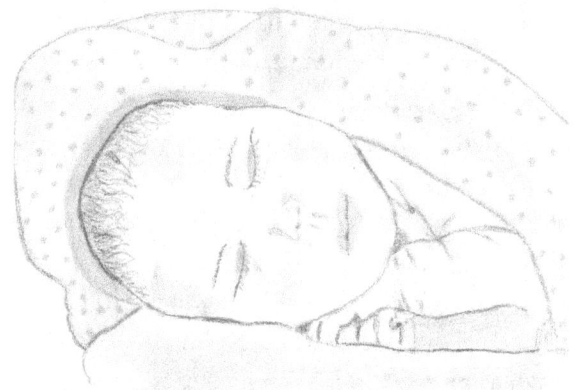

a port? When Nurse Angie calls from day-surgery on February twenty-two, our conversation has nothing to do with travel, cruise ships, or exotic destinations. For better or worse, I'll soon be paddling my way to a local hospital, where my surgeon will install a medical port. In the months to come, this miracle device will be used to draw blood and to deliver the fluids and chemotherapy drugs needed to trounce the intruder that has taken up residence in my right breast.

Angie's voice has an appealing rasp that comforts me. We

cover all of the necessaries, including insurance coverage, medications I am taking, arrival time, night before/morning of pre-surgical shower and germ killing soap instructions — yadda, yadda, yadda — and then Angie reaches through the airwaves to comfort my jittery soul.

"I want you to know that I am a breast cancer survivor," she shares, "as are a number of other nurses who work here. I promise that you will be in good hands. I've worked for this medical provider for over thirty years. I am familiar with the quality of care... This is where I **chose** to be treated."

I send up a silent prayer — *Please let Angie be one of my surgical nurses!*

Before hanging up, with the humor of one who's been there and made it through, she teases, "Now remember — no eating after midnight. Only clear liquids until four hours before the procedure. No lotions, deodorant, or jewelry. Come like the day you were born, but clothed."

As scheduled, I present myself at day surgery. A button-down flannel and loose pants cover my dry, itchy, sterilized birthday suit. Although I do not see Angie, true to her word, I am cared for with respect, skill, and kindness. As my rolling bed wheels through massive double doors to the operating room, tears sting the backs of my eyelids. I don't have time to sort out whether my body's response is rooted in fear or acceptance.

Medical staff transfers me from the rolling bed onto the surgical table. The anesthesiologist covers my mouth with a mask and advises me to take deep breaths. One... two... I am no longer conscious.

With no sense of time, I awake to the sound of two men clearing their throats through the curtains on both sides of me. I understand. My throat feels rough and scratchy, too.

I'm given some time to wake up in the recovery area before I'm wheeled back to my room. There I gobble graham crackers and guzzle water through a straw as if I've just crossed the desert on a camel. I would kill for a burger, fries, and a chocolate malt, which is exactly what my husband makes sure I get on the way home from the hospital.

I've sailed through another cancer adventure. The unrelenting tide of treatment waves carries on with an abdominal MRI, labwork, and chemo-class scheduled the next day. The biggest *scaries* of all will drop on the third of March.

Hello, Taxol, Carboplatin, and Pembrolizumab.

How are we going to play together?

We either make ourselves miserable, or we make ourselves strong. The amount of work is the same.

~ Carlos Castaneda

19

THE CONCERT

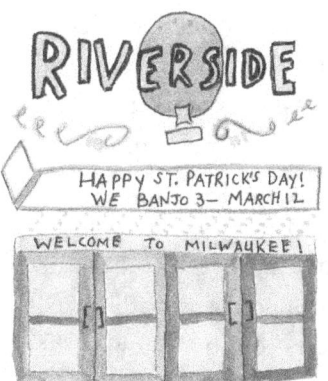

The groupies in front of me stand... What choice do I have? I want to see, so I ignore the historic theater's red velvet fold-down seat, which grazes the backs of my thighs as I stand along with them. I've been listening to the Galway-based band via music apps for several years. Their unique sound, with one foot in Ireland and another in Americana, invites my toes to tap while soulful lyrics carry my faith and trust to a higher plane.

Hours before, my husband skillfully navigated quiet downtown streets, located the parking garage, and squeezed our SUV between two white pavement markings. We walked to a favorite restaurant that serves Napoletana pizzas. Seated at the bar, my tongue explored a couple of mouth ulcers while I sipped an Italian beer and watched Chef Gino paddle pies in and out of their 900-degree wood-fired oven. My taste buds and intestines were not operating at optimum capacity. I refused to let that hamper my enjoyment, managing to eat two of the four triangles on my plate.

Our bellies full and concert-ready, we delivered cardboard-boxed leftovers to our colder-than-a-refrigerator truck and walked a few blocks in the other direction, to the show's venue. While we waited for our ticket barcodes to be scanned, I sucked on a steady stream of lemon drops to alleviate the unnatural and indescribable taste in my mouth.

Tickets to the show were on my Christmas list. Santa came through with passes and parking, foretelling a four-leaf-clover story just days before the celebration of St. Patrick. On Christmas morning, I was gleeful at the prospect of jigging, clapping, and stamping along with an Irish quartet in March. What the jolly old elf did not know is that on March 12, I'd be two days past my second chemotherapy infusion.

I wear the band's name on my chest — a black, green and orange t-shirt bearing the song titles from the group's fifth album. As they play and entertain, I fancy their showmanship is directed at me, knowing full well it is for everyone in attendance. I stand and sway, stamp and clap. Rhythms cover my flesh with *godbumps* and beats prick tears at the backs of my eyelids.

Singing along with *Light in the Sky*, I recognize that an

unknown measure of my future elicits an intensity of feeling I've never experienced before.

This was my earliest awareness that cancer carries cancer gifts.

Just because things hadn't gone the way I planned didn't necessarily mean they had gone wrong.

~Ann Patchett

20

WIZARDRY

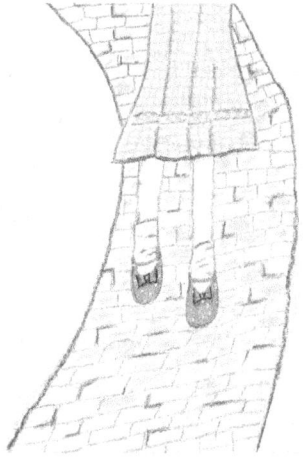

*H*er feet are laced in running shoes, yet the tattoo on the inside of her forearm reminds me of ruby-red slippers.

On the day of my third chemotherapy infusion, I find comfort in a familiar routine. After checking in at the lobby kiosk, I ascend via elevator to the second floor. There, I verify my name and birthdate with a receptionist who attaches a barcoded bracelet around my wrist and advises me to take a seat. Next, I cozy up to the fireplace and wait for my name to be called.

Today, I barely have time to connect to Wi-Fi before I'm beckoned to have my port needle inserted. I remind myself to uncross my legs and to place both feet on the floor for better flow. This particular day — St. Patrick's Day — I carry the luck of the Irish. My blood counts fall within the acceptable range to support benevolent poisoning and the nurse who ~~drinks~~ draws my crimson fluid gives me way more than she takes.

The printed script on her arm is partially covered by her shirt.

"Can I see?" I ask.

Nikki extends her arm, pulls her sleeve above her elbow, and makes it possible for me to read her ink.

You've always had the power my dear, you just had to learn it yourself.

"My grandmother loves this quote from *The Wizard of Oz* and... I guess I do, too." She gives me a wink. "Okay — deep breath in."

The needle penetrates as I exhale. While three vials fill, Nikki and I talk about the many ways I can take care of myself during treatment: diet, exercise, sunshine — uplifting influences.

Because all that separates us from other patients is a curtain, I whisper, "The nurse who gave me my chemo floor tour... I can't remember her name... she was..." I hesitate, "I didn't feel any warmth or possibility from her. After she showed me around and went through paperwork listing every possible chemo side effect, I left the clinic feeling like a week-old helium balloon. I'm just wondering... out loud... if somebody else should give the tours? Somebody encouraging?"

Nikki raises her eyebrows, and even though we are masked, I can tell the corners of her mouth follow suit. "What I'll tell you is that some cancer patients make it to the other side of treatment healthier than they come in. What happens on the outside matters — of course it does — but the shifts you make on the inside is where your true power lies."

The most authentic thing about us is our capacity to create, to overcome, to endure, to love and to be greater than our suffering.

~ Ben Okri

21

SHEAR

arch 2022...
The week after my second chemotherapy infusion, I started a new habit — hair tugging.

My oncologist, Nurse Addie, the printed pages in my cancer binder — all concur that hair begins to drop about two weeks after the first dose.

On Monday, I'm still a brunette with blonde highlights while bowling with my friend Donna.

tug, tug, tug

On Tuesday, I see a woman at the grocery wearing a head covering that looks identical to one I received as a gift. I have an instant feeling of... Pity? Camaraderie? I hate the hat that screams *cancer patient.*

tug, tug, tug

On Wednesday, I participate in two video calls and enjoy lunch with a friend.

tug, tug, tug

On St. Patrick's Day, I draw a German Shepherd holding a shamrock in its teeth for Nurse Nikki while I am infused. I ask Nurse Lisa, *Maybe I'm an exception?*
Maybe you are — shrug.
On Friday, I nap a lot. In the late afternoon, I sit in my studio's burgundy wing chair, reading.

tug —

A collection of brownish-blondish strands... *I am NOT an exception!* I can't stop tugging. I pile my shed onto the desktop next to my seat.

tug, pile — tug, pile — tug, pile

I had my last haircut in early February. After my diagnosis, I reached out to my friend and stylist Erica, sharing my news and canceling my March appointment.

Will you shave my head when it's time?

Yes, of course I will.

While I tug and pile, I do my best to stay present with the book I'm reading, but an internal debate is capturing my concentration.

Am I ready to let my hair go?

Is it time to reach out to Erica?

It's one thing to be sick, quite another to look the part.

Pull the bandage!

Mid-evening I send a photo of hair strands held between my thumb and index to Erica.

It's time.

She replies in a hair's width.

Can you come tomorrow morning at 8:30?

On the drive to the salon, I play my you've-got-this playlist and engage in positive self-talk.

I'm courageous, taking my shearing with a stoic expression. I offer an occasional fake-it-till-you-feel-it smile. Deed done,

Erica refuses payment and gives me a hug so fierce and warm that I resolve to be back in her chair as soon as possible. I'm going to miss our monthly dates.

I am an explorer on an emotional expedition of hills and valleys; approaching appointments with dread and stoicism. I always manage to hold myself together until I get out of the door, then shed a tear or two before I start dismantling and reconstructing the story I am telling myself.

This is happening for *me, not* to *me.*

Once home, I stare at myself in the mirror. I put on a smile and take a selfie. Another big-scary met and survived.

May 2023...

Soft piano accompanies the video.

I hit *replay* again and again.

I cannot hear what the young barber says to the woman whose head he shaves. She looks courageous, taking her shearing with a stoic expression. And then the young man pauses his work before placing the clipper at his own forehead and running it over his crown to the nape of his neck. The cancer patient protests as his beautiful dark hair falls to the floor, mingling with her own. He shaves his entire head despite her insistence that he stop.

Another stylist walks over to the chair. A few inaudible words pass between the barbers.

Has he asked to have his head shaved, too?

The fortress in the chair can no longer hold... She rubs away her tears with the backs of her hands.

A third raven-hair, holding his scissors, steps away from the client in his chair. Like a combine harvesting wheat, the shaver leaves straight exposed scalp rows where hair once stood.

I comment on the post.

This is SO relatable! Just last year my stylist shaved MY head. When I got home I found this photo (below) in my texts. Thank you for posting. I am touched.

Keep going!

Anyone can be confident with a full head of hair. But a confident bald [wo]man - there's your diamond in the rough.

~ Larry David

22

ON REPEAT

*A*lyse is young. Long chestnut hair frames her clear skin. She has a shapely nose and bright eyes. She could be a cover model... if she weren't already a genetic counselor. She introduces herself and asks if I've brought along the forms she sent me weeks ago. I have. I completed the family cancer history to the best of my ability with the help of my sister. I had decided long ago that cancer was not a welcome guest in my body, so when my father shared news of relatives taking up arms against deviant cells, I only listened with half of one ear.

At the infusion bay, I pull the paperwork from my floral satchel and hand it to Alyse from my heated recliner. Together we review the details of who had what. The list is long and my details are sketchy. Sweet as she is, I wish Alyse would atomize and let me get back to my drawing.

Alyse is enthusiastic about her work, and the power, she believes, comes from knowing about one's genetic markers. I am a hard sell, leaning toward *ignorance is bliss*.

During our time together, I learned that my blood can be tested for over a hundred cancer-related genetic markers. Approximately thirteen percent of all cancers are hereditary. I've got my Benadryl on board. Paying attention is a struggle as words like mutation, variant, one-hit cell, two-hit cell, and health-insurance genetic discrimination pass between us. Alyse knows her material and advocates for more testing rather than less, in a non-pushy way.

"You have up to three months to decide which alterations you'd like to be tested for."

Coming into this conversation, I'd already decided to be tested for the BRCA1 and BRCA2 genes as that knowledge will guide surgical decisions around partial mastectomy, full mastectomy, or double mastectomy.

"Three months? Okay. Please submit for BRCA1 and 2 right now. I'd like to sort out my feelings about additional genetic exploration."

Alyse smiles. "Of course! That's fine. I'll make a note to reach back out to you in a month. By then, you will have the BRCA results."

"Thank you."

I stuff the paper she's given me into my three-ring cancer-care binder's front pocket and shelve the matter for another day.

———

True to her word, Alyse sent me an email message a month later. "Hi Gail. I'm following up to see if you'd like additional testing. With your family's history of colorectal cancer, I strongly recommend further investigation there. Also, I suggest you consider looking for evidence of uterine and ovarian genetic alteration."

After our initial meeting, I discussed my reluctance for further testing with my parrot — I mean myself.

> *Me: Do I really want to know if I'm predisposed?*
> *Parrot: Do I really want to know? Squawk!*
> *Me: If I worry too much, will my faulty parts get*
>   *cancer because I believe they're going to?*
> *Parrot: Worry too much! Don't know! Don't know!*
> *Me: The testing is already paid for...*
> *Parrot: Paid for! Paid for! It's only money! Aaaack!*
> *Me: Thanks. You can go now.*
> *Parrot: Go now! You can go now!*

I reply to Alyse: "Hi Alyse! Sure. Go ahead with the ones you recommend. Nothing more. Gail"

When the results arrive, I'm surprised that all but two are... negative! The two that are not negative are not positive either. They are called uncertain variants which means... nobody knows for sure... the definition of *uncertain*.

Parrot? I call, *We're good.*
We're good! Squawk! We're good!

We ARE good.
Growing stronger with each decision... and action.

Your genetics is not your destiny.
    ~ George M. Church

23

RAINBOW HAIR

$\mathcal{S}$pring sunshine warms my shoulders as I cross the parking lot to enter the clinic's vestibule through sliding glass doors. Inside the cancer clinic's lobby, I pull a surgical mask from a cardboard box and slip its elastic bands behind my ears. I'm aware of a man with young children, sitting by the windows, on modern gray furniture. I wonder what their business is here on a Thursday morning — this place where patients come to reclaim their lives from mutant cells. The curiosity washes through me as fast as it appears. I have my own page to keep my eyes on.

At the kiosk, I enter my name and phone number, submit that I've not left the country since my last visit, and confirm that my insurance information has not changed and that indeed I am here to be infused with miracle poison that will keep my life moving in a healthier direction.

Despite circumstance, my black Mary Jane shoes hold sprightly feet. I've made a decision to dress for success, believing cancer will show more respect to a warrior wearing clothes that mean business than to a *grump dressed in frump*, sporting dirty sneakers.

Still trying to work out exactly what to do with my newly bald head, the day's experiment involves a five-foot-long scarf wrapped and knotted with the aid of a purple rubberband. Teal, yellow, red, green, and purple fuse themselves into abstract flowers and butterflies. The choice feels gaudy... over-done... and yet bold in a way I'd never have tried without cancer's nudge.

As I finish up proffering my credit card for co-payment, I hear an angelic voice from behind. The child says something my heart longs to hear.

"Daddy — Look!" exclaims the young girl at my back. "She has rainbow hair!"

And before I have a chance to form a response, I hear her father shush her as they exit through the sliding glass doors. In the eyes of a child, I am not sick or garish... I am beautiful.

Did her father not hear the gift his daughter had just given me?

I look down at my wrist. A friend, whose brilliant awareness understands that I need empowerment more than sympathy, sent me a cuff bracelet inscribed with inspiration:

Your life.
Your canvas.
Paint it with purpose.
Paint it brilliant.

———————

My mission in life is not merely to survive, but to thrive; and to do so with some passion, some compassion, some humor, and some style.

~ Maya Angelou

24

WHAT A GIRL WANTS

*D*id you ever bring donuts to work?

When I was a twenty-something with an office job, precedent encouraged birthday boys and girls to bring in enough frosting and glaze to feed their fellows. As a huge fan of fried dough, I bit into this tradition with enthusiasm. Almost weekly there was a caramel long John, frosted cinnamon roll, or apple turnover to sweeten my coffee break.

Decades later, my only officemate has four legs and wears a fur coat year round. She never brings donuts to work and makes me take walks instead. Though my sweet tooth laments, my heart, waistline, and dentist are fans of the shift.

How many donuts does it take to make a girl happy?

So far... I know it's more than five. Better that I'm not tempted.

It just so happens that I'm scheduled for a chemotherapy infusion on my birthday! Aware weeks in advance, I send a text to my niece in Texas, whose baking and decorating skills rival Parisian pastry chefs.

> Hey! How are you? I have a question — hoping for a "yes" but will take "no" as a complete sentence — no hurt feelings. I have a chemo infusion on my birthday and would love to bring your cutout cookies as a treat for my caregivers. You can choose the design... thinking pastel for spring? I'm a paying customer... not asking for a freebie. <3 Love you!

The day before my birthday-infusion, our postal carrier hands over the cardboard-boxed bounty. I bring it inside, slice through the packing tape, and one by one, pull cupcake-shaped cutouts from a dense nest of paper shreds. Not one of the thirty gems shows any sign of wear or tear from its cross-country travel.

I *ooh* and *aah* to myself and anyone else within earshot. I send a few pictures to our family and post a couple of images on social media. I'm awed by the craftsmanship and cannot wait to share. A rummage through the attic cubby of holiday decorations scores an Easter basket that I fill and arrange with care. My joy in this opportunity to be the birthday bearer of glad tidings is all the gift I want... with one small exception.

"Please," I pray, "Please God... Make my blood rich and healthy."

Today is meant to be my ninth of twelve Taxol and Carbo-platin administrations. My neutrophils and platelets have failed us twice. On weeks six and seven I was sent home without treatment because of low counts.

I don't want to be a failure on my birthday.

How about if my birthday gift is meaty blood, so that we can keep the chemo train moving up the tracks?

C'mon God, let's make this infusion a go!

A friend once told me God always answers — yes, no, or maybe.

On my birthday, the answer is a resounding *no*.

I'm in the heated recliner when Nurse Addie delivers the news. The sky is blue. The sun is shining. Geese and cranes enjoy the pond outside the window. I'm all dressed up with a big, fat *not-happening-today-kid* on my bloodwork report.

Addie removes my port needle. "I'm going to call your oncologist. We need to see about getting you started on neutrophil boosting shots. If he agrees, we'll need to get approval from your insurance. Sit tight. I'll start making calls. Hopefully, we can give your first shot today so that your counts are up for next Thursday."

Addie has been my lead nurse at every infusion. I'd follow her anywhere. She's smart, efficient, kind, and an advocate for her patients. I pull the handle to raise the recliner's footrest, extract my pencils and sketchbook from my cancer bag, and play uplifting music through my airpods.

I can't say exactly why, but this inability to receive chemo feels like a foot extended to trip me when I'm already barely moving along. I suspect it's because we have a plan to hit the cancer hard and fast and now my body isn't cooperating. I understand and trust that the doctor is taking a big picture / whole body view. I have little doubt that this will all work itself out in the long run — it's just that being thrust back into the unknown again feels unsettling. My challenge continues to be focusing on the light instead of the dark.

The chemo bay is full and active today. The nursing crew waltzes in time to beeps, alarms, and calls. Quite content with my music and art, I'm unaware and unconcerned about how much time has passed.

Addie stops by my makeshift studio. "Thank you for the cookies. I didn't have breakfast today, and they are keeping me going. Beautiful, too! Sorry this is taking so long. Dr. S has approved and put in the order for shots. We're waiting to hear from the insurance. It was sent as a priority request, but they still have twenty-four hours to answer. I'm hoping somebody picks it up soon."

"No worries. I kinda like it here." I smile.

Ping.

A text from my friend pops up.

> I was sitting here and thinking and praying about your two delayed treatments on this Holy Thursday… I always want answers to "why"… why wasn't my prayer for your treatment answered… but then God pointed out to me what an amazing inspirational gift you are who has the strength to write, illustrate, and share your journey with all of us in spite of whatever kind of day you're experiencing — that makes me appreciate more than ever the gift of today. That's the answer to my question and I said a prayer of thanks.

> Reading this gave me godbumps and inspired my heart and faith to grow. I am loved and I am blessed. Can't ask for more than that. Thank you.

Sometimes when we are in the dark, a friend with a flashlight can make all the difference.

Addie appears with a syringe. "Got approval. You get to come back tomorrow for a second dose. And the bright side is — no chemo on your birthday. How are you going to celebrate?"

———

Everything will turn out right, the world is built on that.
~ Mikhail Bulgakov

25

SHOTS

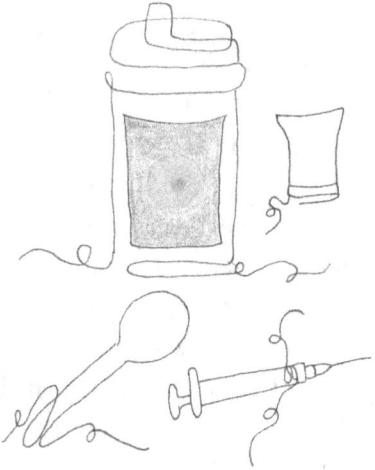

*W*hen you need a boost, how about a few shots?
Not whiskey, tequila, or gin, which lift your spirits for a hot minute only to leave you weighed down like a drawer full of price-thrill orange-tags that you'll never wear.

I'm talking about the clear liquid that's plunged into my bicep. All shots come with their unique set of challenges. From bleeding gums to vomiting, bone pain to — yipes! — paralysis, this pharmaceutical-grade shooter also carries a two-handled bag. Here's the thing: If we don't build my white cell count, I cannot receive chemotherapy, and if I don't receive chemotherapy, what's gonna outgun the mutiny on my bounty?

It's three in the morning. I wake up in an unfamiliar bed to a strange sensation in my rib cage. Ah, yes... I'm in a hotel room in the upper tip of Lower Michigan. There's a wedding today, and I've yet to decide how I'll cover my head to match my dress. I have the first two shots of white-cell-boosting magic potion on board, and my body is... adjusting? During yesterday's six-hour drive from home to here, whizzing past a billboard war between legal drugs and addiction support services, I felt a few twinges, popped a few tablets for pain, and got on with living. These early morning sensations are different. I decide not to classify what I feel as pain. I stay curious and settle on *mini-fireworks between vertebrae and ribs* as my writerly metaphor.

I pop a few more tablets and enjoy the show.

Around seven, room and sky still dark, I want coffee. The little pot in our room looks iffy. I pull on sweats, boots, and parka and slip out the door so as not to wake my sleeping husband. The mini-fireworks and I embrace a caffeine adventure. We cross a filled-to-capacity parking lot to a cluster of quaint buildings. There are a few shops, a pub, and a restaurant — all closed. We head off to the hotel's main lobby, where there's a chain coffee shop whose acidic brew is on my *do not drink* list. I stand blinking at the board.

"What is a latte? Is it sweet?"

A woman in a black apron, whose expression screams, *I'd rather be anywhere than here*, replies, "Steamed milk poured over a shot of espresso. You can add flavored syrup if you want it sweet."

"Okay. I'll have that. The biggest one. No syrup."

Another *shot*... We've got a theme going here!

Turns out I like the new-to-me joe. I like it a latte — and wear a frothy mustache in support of adventure.

The wedding turns out to be great fun. I even get out for a twirl or two on the dance floor. The mini-fireworks fascinate without setting any fires. I enjoy a second latte on Sunday before we trek past the billboard war on our way home.

I continue to receive shots for the duration of my chemo-therapy infusions. My body acclimates to the drug, and mini-fireworks are few and far between.

———

One morning I shot an elephant in my pajamas. How he got into my pajamas I'll never know.

~ Groucho Marx

26

THOSE EYES

𝒩o stir stick.
No maraschino cherries.
Not an olive in sight.

And yet... an antihistamine cocktail circulates through my system, unhinging my inhibitions.

Nurse Katarina is my mixologist.

Throughout today's infusion, she monitors beeps, drips, and my well-being.

I pull pencils and drawing paper from my flowered satchel.

I send out silent gratitude for heated blankets, heated recliners with movable tray tables, and the kindness of caregivers.

I sketch a bunny for Katarina, whose belly bump speaks of upcoming maternity leave.

The child is her first.

A girl.

She'll be named Madesyn.

I search the world wide web for quotes to empower new parents, then weave the wise words into the white spaces around the rabbit. Carl Sandburg's, "A baby is God's opinion that life should go on," hugs bunny ears that stand ready for whatever needs to be heard.

When a hanging bag runs dry and an alarm sounds, Katarina comes to hook up my next drink. My well-practiced timidity is nowhere to be found.

If I wasn't a middle-aged woman in chemo bay five, being cared for by a young expectant mother...

"You have the most beautiful eyes I have ever seen."

One might think I'd just tossed out a pick up line in a bar.

After the syllables flow through my lips, I feel awkward and embarrassed. I cannot pinpoint a single reason for my bashful feelings. My admiration is heartfelt, honest, and authentic.

Where did I pick up a belief that sharing words of love with acquaintances is perverse?

And how will I see differently going forward?

I'm certain to find a way.

The truth is, once you learn how to die, you learn how to live.

~ Mitch Albom

27

HOLY HUNGER

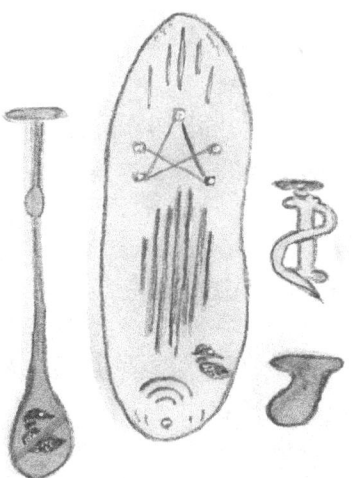

S   *tand-up paddling targets muscles all over the body. From toes to the brain's neural pathways, the entire tapestry of the body is engaged.*

In the heart of summer, a friend sends a photo of his young sons hefting backpacks containing inflatable paddleboards. My curiosity is piqued.

I've tried the sport twice. The first time, I paddled for a couple hundred feet before splashing off to give the next person in line a turn. I felt unstable and lacked confidence... and the voices in my head were cacophonous. I fretted over my middle-aged self looking like a fool.

In contrast, a few years later, my second stand-up water paddle fed my confidence. Supportive friends, who were also learners, sailed with me. The evening was warm and the lake calm. My confidence burgeoned one stroke at a time. The growth experience left me craving more, but with a home surrounded by dry land and a vehicle challenge to transport a seven-foot-plus board, the only opportunity I saw was to cross my fingers and hope to be invited back to the lake house.

Until... I saw those shiny, happy little people in the photo.

> *Do I have agency?*
> *Can I lead myself?*
> *Can I... purchase, transport, inflate, and balance?*
> *Can I feed my soul's desire to grow?*

Where there's a will, there's a way.
I start asking my friend questions:

> *Where did you purchase the boards?*
> *Are they stable?*
> *Are they expensive?*
> *Would you recommend one for a friend?*

He sends along a link to a website that kicks off an internal battle.

It costs too much.

We have cancer... Seriously?

We don't know how to inflate/deflate/launch/stop/turn — *aak!* Looks intimidating!

If we never try things we don't know how to do, how will we ever get to do them?

What if we float a few times and grow bored?

Stop. Go away!

For days I visit the website. I watch the company's instructional videos as my incisors peel flesh from fruit, noting that my beloved Bing cherries taste like cough medicine. I ping-pong back and forth over the net as the sale price comes, goes, and comes back again.

When I can't stand my energy-robbing indecision any longer, I leap and hit the BUY NOW button.

As our delivery man leaves in his big brown truck, I tear into the cardboard box with my name on it. All of the pieces are present: board, two-piece paddle, mega hand pump, and safety strap. Sweat drips onto our concrete drive as I pump my heart into a frenzy, practicing set up and take down before making my big splash at a local lake. I'm grateful to be two weeks past my most recent chemo infusion because I feel well and ready.

I dress, pack, and prepare for my first voyage. The evening is warm. The lake is calm. My confidence is... a bit shaky. I talk to myself as if I'm encouraging a friend.

You've got this!

What's the worst that can happen?

So what if you fall in and get wet?

Pumping up the board takes a lot of oomph. I rest as needed. I'm exhilarated when I wade into the shallow water — alone in my awkwardness — which is just how I like it. First, I sit. Next, I wobble onto my knees and paddle around a bit.

Muscles I didn't even know I had clench and twitch. Eventually, I stand on legs full of jelly and cling to the shoreline as I make my way forward.

By the end of summer, I paddle like Pocahontas, able to ride boat wakes without dropping to my knees.

I've heard people say that what is small to the bear looms large to the ant.

Purchasing a paddle board and sailing off into the waves as a cancer patient empowers me.

Never once do I feel like a fool in my tankini and headscarf.

> *I feel alive.*
> *I feel steady.*
> *I feel free.*
> *My hunger is satisfied.*

I cannot count the good people I know who, to my mind, would be even better if they bent their spirits to the study of their own hungers.

~ M.F.K. Fisher

28

SOUND OF MUSIC

*a*n angel bowls a solid strike.

      Lightning flashes in celebration.

Henrietta pants and paces.

The sixty-five-pound *fourleg* climbs into my lap, steps on my sensitivities, and hops off to resume her patrol of the windows.

Whimpers and whines play on my nerves.

"Do you want to go outside, Hen?"

She trots to the door with a slight wag of her tail.

I don a neon-teal, polyvinyl-chloride rainsuit that I purchased years ago for just such occasions. The elastic waist is snug. *Oh well... I'm in.* I shrug and the noise from my clownish attire assaults my ears. We head out into a wind that drives horizontal drops.

Henrietta leads me to the top of a grass-covered hill that leads down to a thicket of overgrown brambles. She's solid. Her gaze into the darkness does not waver. She no longer pants or paces. I turn my back to the wind and wonder why she's more comfortable out in the elements than inside where it's warm and dry.

I tug on her leash and she obliges.

"Go potty!" I encourage, wanting to go back in.

Henny prefers to be out-of-doors.

She strolls as if we're on a sunny Sunday park exploration.

I begin to sing... loud.

"When you walk through a storm, hold your head up high, and don't be afraid of the dark!"

Henny squats and empties her bladder.

"At the end of the storm is a golden sky and the sweet silver song of a lark."

We enter through the laundry room.

I slip out of the dripping gear, towel Henrietta from snout to tail, toss her a treat, and return to the recliner.

The crashes and flashes eb as the storm moves east.

Henrietta curls up on the carpet and snores lightly.

Her paws and tail dream-twitch.

This storm has passed.

Under my fleece blanket, I contemplate how music holds and empowers me through the hue and cry of cancer treatment. The playlist started with a song link sent by a friend.

Darling, darling... You're beautiful... Gotta keep your head up! Never let anything bring you down; sunshine will always come around. Stay strong; move on. You have such a beautiful soul.
("Darling" by Beautiful Chorus)

As friends and the great mystery bring tunes and lyrics into my awareness, I give them my heart, adding them to an ever-growing musical mix.

While driving myself to a chemotherapy infusion, I harmonize my voice with Rising Appalachia:

I am resilient. I trust the movement,
I negate the chaos — uplift the negative!

On the drive home, I'm a badass with Christina Aguilera singing "Fighter":

Made me learn a little bit faster. Made my skin a little bit thicker.
Makes me that much smarter — so thanks for making me a fighter!

The playlist is sixty-seven songs strong and still growing. I'm grateful for the musicians and lyricists who've helped me create a mindset that supports strength and flourishing.

See, C?

I'm not alone.

Even the musicians are pulling for me.

———

I love the way music inside a car makes you feel invisible; if you play the stereo at max volume, it's almost like other people can't see into your vehicle. It tints your windows, somehow.

~ Chuck Klosterman

29

PICKING

*W*ith purpose, I pull the navy, cotton bandanna from a pile of flowered, polka-dotted, and paisley satins. My faded selection has made no less than forty circles around the sun. The scarf once belonged to my cancer-fighting mother, who used it to cover her bald head.

Shortly after my cancer diagnosis, I searched for a Polaroid snapshot that lived in my mind's eye. I found it in a heavy cardboard box, inside a family-heirloom chest. In the photo, Mom

sits at my grandmother's kitchen table, dressed in a pink flow-
ered button-down, topped off with a snow white cardigan.
March 26, 1978 is penned in smudged red ink below the image.
She wears the navy bandanna as part of her ensemble.

I wonder at the mystery... *Why on earth did I hang onto that
bandanna for all of these years? Is it because it's one of the few pieces
of my mother that I can touch and hold?* The only other tangible
object I can think of is a vintage hair brush and mirror set.
Sometime in my teens I carelessly left the mirror on my
unmade bed, sat on the glass, and cracked it, then spent countless hours worrying about the seven years of bad luck to follow.

I choose to believe the time and energy I spent persever-
ating about things that never came to pass has value —
contributing to the person I am today. And yet going forward, I
vow to pedal through life's tricky bits with faith that I am riding
in tandem with a higher power. There's no room for worry in
our baskets or satchels.

It's a perfect day to spend in a strawberry field. Under a hazy
sky, I drive north on quiet roads. The radio announcer forecasts
temperatures in the upper seventies with increasing peeks of
sunshine as morning slides into afternoon. Arriving at my destina-
tion, I'm greeted by acres of evenly-spaced, rich-green rows. I spy
my dad's pickup truck across the fields. Its driver stands under a
pop-up tent, talking with workers who run the self-pick operation.

I park, hop out of my truck, and cross the distance to where
I can give my dad a big hug. Feeling well enough to spend a
couple of hours plucking ripe reds from lush plants is mean-
ingful for several reasons. First, chemotherapy is not holding
me back from living life like I expected it would. Second, the
opportunity to pick next to my eighty-five-year-old dad — to
hear his childhood *5-cents-for-each-bushel-picked* stories — is
something I do not want to take for granted. And third, I can
enjoy all the sun-warmed berries I care to eat... no charge!

The field manager tells us he's going to set us up to harvest an unpicked parcel down the road. Over the course of a decade or more, my dad and Acario have built a friendship. Acario is well aware that my dad has a preference for the freezer-friendly Honeoye variety. He's intent on giving the man what he wants. Last year, I watched Acario, who picks at lightning speed, toss handfuls of fruit into my dad's cardboard flat. Then, like a mother hen, he watched my father step over the rows heading back to the tent. His concern was not for the berry plants, but rather for his picking pal.

Back when the snow still flew and berries were a spring dream, it was my dad whose world I feared shaking the most with news of my diagnosis. He'd already lost his wife to lung cancer, his father to throat cancer, and countless friends and relatives to abnormal cells. Ten years prior to my breast biopsy, he fretted and felt helpless as my sister was treated with a mastectomy, chemotherapy, and radiation. *Did I want to be strong for someone else?* More than anything, I want to show my dad I can weather whatever cancer throws at me, writing a different story for our family.

We crawl along together on our hands and knees. When we decide we have enough berries in our baskets, we load the flats into the truck's bed and drive back to the tent for weighing and paying. I suspect that sometime over the next twenty-four hours, one of us will call the other to share the news that our bounty is washed, hulled, and in the freezer. Likely dad will tell me about the baking soda biscuits he's made to top with his juicy prize and whipping cream. Simple traditions carry such joy.

On this June day, I am alive and strong, choosing to be a mirror of possibility.

Thanks, Mom, for lending me your blue bandanna.

Dad said I have your grit.

I can't imagine anything he might have said that would have warmed my heart more.

———

A tree is known by its fruit; a man by his deeds. A good deed is never lost; he who sows courtesy reaps friendship, and he who plants kindness gathers love.

~ Saint Basil

30

RED LIGHT — GREEN LIGHT

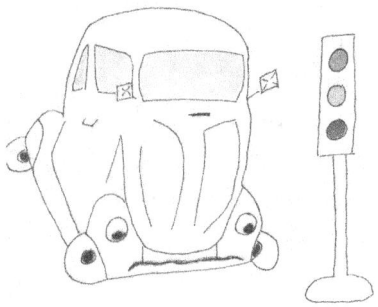

*F*riday.

I'm showered, packed, and ready for our weekend getaway. My partial mastectomy is scheduled for Tuesday. The hospital requires a pre-procedure — negative COVID test.

So... while my husband walks Henrietta and readies himself, I turn up the volume on my cancer playlist, drive to the designated clinic, pull into a reserved swab spot, and call the number on the sign so that a gowned and masked caregiver can pop out to swab my nostrils.

"Good morning! My name is Gail — Boenning, B-O-E-N-N-I-N-G. I have a 9:30 appointment for a COVID test."

I hear breathing and tapping.

The pause is long.

Too long.

"Oh! I see why I couldn't find you. You're scheduled for tomorrow. The test has to take place within seventy-two hours of your surgery."

Confusion rides the cell connection and pinballs through my synapses. Panic takes up residence in the V of my rib cage along with a hundred and one thoughts and feelings — shame, blame, how, now what, and *Darn it, Gail! How'd you mess this up?* race through my neural pathways before I speak.

"Tomorrow?" I squeak. "But I'm going out of town today. I won't be home until Sunday evening."

"I can swab you today if your surgeon waives the seventy-two-hour requirement, but... you'll have to contact their office, and they'll need to send me an amended order."

Thoughts swirl like water going down a drain.

Should I just stay home? I don't want to be a bother. Do I have the clinic's number? I've really been anticipating this trip... and friends are traveling to meet us. There's only one thing for it. I must try!

"Okay." My internal battle rages. Do I shrink away, or do I amend my calendar misstep? "Do I need to move my car?"

"Yup. Please take a spot in the general lot." Compassion blooms via her tone. "Hope to see you back again this morning!"

I back up, pull forward, find a new slot, take a breath, and regroup.

Think; think; think.

What's your next step?

I believe life has abundant patience for those who remain calm.

And just like that, I know who to contact.

I find my nurse navigator's number in my contacts and touch the green dot circling a telephone receiver.

"Hi Gem. This is Gail Boenning. I'm in the parking lot of the COVID test site and it seems... I've made a mistake. I thought my appointment was today, but it's actually tomorrow. I'm wondering if you can help? I have plans to be out of town for the weekend. How do you suggest I proceed? The nurse said she can swab me today if my surgeon waives the seventy-two-hour requirement. Can you help? I'll hang out here in the parking lot for a while. I hope you get this message... Call me back."

I touch the red circle to end the call. Within ten minutes, I'm talking with Gem. She will call the surgeon's office on my behalf. *Sit tight and I'll call you back as soon as I have an answer.*

I've turned off the ignition. The sun is shining and my windows are open. I breathe and marvel at my good fortune. Gem continues to be a godsend.

A few minutes later, Gem calls. The seventy-two-hour requirement is waived. I am swabbed and my weekend — pre-surgical getaway — is filled with friendship, delights from the Sweet House bakery, and faith that Tuesday's surgery will bring me one step closer to CURE.

If you are the kind of person who is waiting for the right thing to happen, you might wait for a long time. It's like waiting for all the traffic lights to be green for five miles before you'll start your trip.

~ Robert Kiyosaki

31

MIRACLES

I'd follow you anywhere.
I want to be you when I grow up.
Can we go clothes shopping together?
Do you carve the meat at your house?

These are thoughts I've had about my surgeon.

Of course I haven't said them out loud to her face.

That'd just be awkward... very much like telling your nurse she has the most beautiful eyes you've ever seen while under the influence of Benadryl.

Instead, my admiration stands tall — shared via words on a page.

Calm, confident, capable, and kind, Dr. P has walked both sides of the physician-patient line.

I heard she's a breast-cancer survivor.

Shared experiences breed understanding.

At almost every visit I have with her, a student trails, observes, and learns.

When she asks me, "Can (student's name) touch?"

I always answer, "Yes," and send up a prayer of gratitude for her generous rippling of her skills.

On the morning of my partial mastectomy, I wrote in my public journal:

I'm ready for today's surgery. I have been paying close attention to the chatter in my mind, and I am delighted to report there has been very little perseveration as to what might or might not happen. I'm taking events as they come and looking at surgery as an adventure.

An adventure?

Is my curiosity bigger than my fear?

When Dr. P meets me in recovery, she tells me everything went well: The initial screening of the three sentinel lymph nodes removed along with the breast tissue reflects no mutant cells. They'll be sent to the lab for further testing… but right now, all signs indicate I have had a complete pathological response.

Several days later, early September 2022, she telephones to confirm I am cancer free.

My surgical wounds heal.

My breast looks very much like it did before the surgery, with a thin scar disguised by the areola.

Everything I thought cancer would be and what my experience is are two different things.

I continue to find the gifts in the lessons.

We think of a miracle, such as a sudden healing, as an event. Actually, the real miracle is not the event, but how we perceive the event in our lives. Ask yourself which is the real miracle: when the check finally arrives, the deadline is extended, the lawsuit is settled, the exception is made? Or when you cope, serene and smiling, in the face of unbearable circumstances, triumphantly blowing everybody's mind—including your own—with your poise and courage?

~ Sarah Ban Breathnach

32

INKED

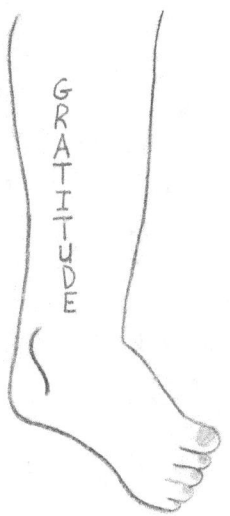

"They're fine for anybody who wants one, or many... I just don't want one for me. They're so permanent and...I like to change my mind. Tattoos aren't like jewelry or scarves that you can put on and take off. And what happens when my skin starts to sag? Eww!"

For many years, this was my thought pattern around inked body images.

Then one summer day on vacation, a friend and I left our kids and husbands at our little rented cabin in the woods while we trekked into a town full of tourist traps. The sign outside the tattoo shop advertised henna designs for $15.00.

In recent years, I had noticed fellow yoga students with small body markings — a lotus on a shoulder blade, a butterfly perched on a collar bone, a symbol of yin/yang on a bicep. A woman from my book club had recently visited India and returned home with an intricate henna floral design on the back of her hand. She explained that henna is temporary, lasting no more than a week or two.

"Do you want to get a henna tattoo?" I tossed in an inkling of incentive. "My treat!"

"I'll come in with you."

A woman whose arms told stories in full color handed us a book of henna designs available for the promotional price. Small, simple, and sparse options suited my sensibilities. My friend and I each made a selection.

As a passenger on the drive back to the lake, I delighted in a subtle thrill of exhilaration for stepping outside of the narrow image I held of myself. My eyes traveled again and again to the reddish-brown letters above my exterior right ankle bone.

I cannot say which I loved more; the leap of my rebel spirit or the design I chose.

Before we left the shop, our artist confirmed our adornments would last for about a week *if* we did not spend much time in water. *Well, well, well... Am I done swimming for the rest of this vacation?* By the time I was back in my own bed, GRATITUDE was fading fast but not forgotten.

More than a decade has spun around the clock face since

my singular tattoo experience. Today I'm visiting a new section of the cancer center where I'll be fit for a form-molded cushion to hold my body *just-so* for twirls with radiation equipment. Also, my chest and torso will be marked with tiny dots of permanent ink. Thanks to GRATITUDE, I'm psyched for the dots.

Eeeeee!

Tattoos that will not wash off.

Now my rebel spirit wants an inked image of victory to accentuate my port scar... I'm open to suggestions.

My body is my journal, and my tattoos are my story.

~ Johnny Depp

33

WORTH ANALYSIS

On a hot, humid, late-summer afternoon
My observation is not light and airy.
At first glance it feels oppressive
And kind of scary.

I take time to reflect and breathe.
New perspective rises.
Switching glasses
Yields surprises.

A few days ago, I came across a line from a poem that resonated:

To pay attention, this is our endless and proper work.

I do pay attention to many things outside of myself but have a sense that paying attention to my thoughts and what's inside of me is where my real power lies.

Have you ever thought about that?

Anyhow, this afternoon's experience and self-analysis relates to big c, little c, and no c.

As the music fades for my dance with cancer, I pluck up the courage to login to our medical insurance site. Since February, I've been in and out of the cancer clinic, imaging machines, and the hospital. I'm well aware that my treatment comes with a monetary cost and yet my mailbox has been almost devoid of bills.

For seven months, I've managed to completely ignore the missing fees-for-service... until yesterday's curiosity got the better of me.

When I looked at the claims and payment pages documenting transactions between caregivers and our insurance company, I first felt small and humbled. What rolled in next surprised me...

Shame — *Gail Lynn, shame on you!*

You are not worth that much money!

Hundreds upon hundreds of thousands of dollars!

Spent to save me?

I wouldn't think such a thing about somebody else's cost of care.

Big scary #1 roars in my ears. For so long, I've been a *work-in-progress* with my thoughts around money and spending. Even though I'm now aware that money and value are not the same thing, I still wrestle with the belief that the energy of money is worth more... than the energy of me?

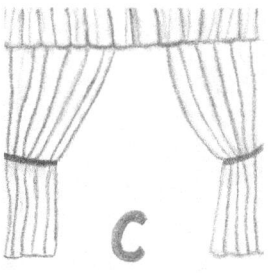

Gulp!

Tears sting the eyes of my soul.

What is a human life worth?

To other humans?

To God/Universe/Higher Power?

Who decides?

I have received many, many cancer gifts since my diagnosis on February, 11, 2022.

I count the experience I just shared and my self-directed questions among the gifts.

I continue to practice my *endless and proper work...* and write a love letter to myself... and to God.

Today's calendar notes: World Gratitude Day

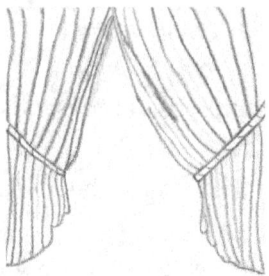

I am grateful for the imperfect systems of healthcare and insurance that preserve my life.

I am grateful for my husband and his employer who make it possible for us to have insurance.

I gratefully unite my internal and external ways of thinking, being, and doing.

I am grateful *you* are here.

Adversity and perseverance and all these things can shape you. They can give you a value and a self-esteem that is priceless.

~ Scott Hamilton

34

FRANCIS

I drink him in — wisps of gray hair cover his age-spotted skull. Bruises, like spilled prune juice, decorate his arms. He sits in front of a wall of false flames that deliver warmth and a pour of comfort into the waiting room. His neck bends forward as his eyes take in whatever his smartphone is delivering, while his feet rest in the stirrups of a wheelchair.

I find him interesting and want to start a conversation, yet my life's experience has taught me to always be polite. *Don't interrupt or make a bother of yourself, Gail Lynn.* I've been fighting against the bars for some time, but on that crisp, cloudy fall morning, the training had caged me.

Taking my favorite tan leather seat close to the fireplace, I pull out my own smartphone, crane my neck into an unhealthy position, and follow the steps needed to access the clinic's WiFi. Sly like a fox, I snap a photo of the fireplace. I want the image for the daily love letter my trio of muses write and publish while today's infusion drips into my system — a miracle medicine that commandeers my body's healthy cells into a peace-keeping force. I'm grateful for immunotherapy, cancer detection equipment, medical personnel, medicinal treatment, and the researchers and scientists who continue their lives of service to help patients like me.

I'm cropping the old man's foot out of my photo when a soft voice touches my ears. "Excuse me? Will you help?" I look up and a mottled hand draws my eye to my fellow's smartphone, now resting on beige carpet squares, between stirrups and wheels. "I can't..."

Before he can finish his sentence, I retrieve his device. Handing it to him, I ask a question that's just plain stupid, pulled from the auto-file of polite niceties. "How are you doing?" As soon as the words are out of my mouth, I catch myself with a *right-hook. Ugh — Gail Lynn! Can't you see he looks like crap? Why didn't you ask something less personal? Like... How about this weather?*

"Not good. Not good at all," he replies. "I have leukemia. They've stopped the chemotherapy... Now I get transfusions every other week to keep me alive. I'm ninety-three and might put a stop to it soon. I've lived a good life. My wife is gone."

Idiot, my inner critic tsk-tsks. *Now what are you gonna reply to THAT?*

Stymied for words, I nod as a sign of understanding. His

ninety-three years of life experience has my back. He continues, "We had six sons."

"Whoa! I only had one... Can't imagine six boys."

"Oh... We had great fun," he replied. "Wisconsin is nice, but we were living in Michigan at the time and... Michigan is better. Every weekend we took a trip to get out and be active in nature."

"What part of Michigan?"

"Dearborn. I worked for Ford Motors at the time."

"Grandchildren?"

"Fifteen... and three great-grands."

A nurse appears and takes a position at the handles of my newfound friend's ride.

"Looks like you're needed," I say to him... And to the nurse, "You're stealing my conversation partner?"

"What a joy it's been getting to know you." I grasp and hold his hand. I've heard it said that *real* love goes beyond feeling and emotion. Real love is core to core attraction — caring about something or someone outside of yourself.

Who is this woman reaching out to touch a stranger? One part of me questions another.

"We haven't exchanged names! I'm Gail."

"Francis," he replies. "My wife's name was Frances, too."

I give his hand a squeeze and then let go.

I smile. "You've made my day. You really have. Best wishes for both of us."

Each friend represents a world in us, a world possibly not born until they arrive, and it is only by this meeting that a new world is born.

~ Anais Nin

35

RADIANT

*M*y salt-and-pepper pixie exposes bare flesh. Sunshine sizzles sweat at the nape. I shift seats, into the shade, then back again after an easterly breeze raises a bounty of *godbumps* across my skin.

In less than a year, I satisfied Dr. S's *Goals of Treatment:* CURE.

I've started to tell people I am *cured.* Every time I say the word out loud, I feel a little like I'm taunting fate. Then I remind myself that fate is for those who ignore their destiny. I am cured because I am destined to take what I learned and make a difference in this world. That's my story and I'm sticking to it.

As my neck broils, fleeting thoughts of sunscreen and skin cancer flutter by. I recall the burning and itching, peeling and cracking, of an irradiated breast. By the time I made it through chemotherapy and surgery — which revealed a complete pathological response — radiation treatment felt like a rule-following exercise... not unlike applying sunscreen to prevent something that might, or might not, ever come to pass.

By the time I'm sliding in and out of the robot-like radiation machine five days a week, I feel this cancerous adventure is already beginning to fade in the rearview mirror. I continue to find joy in the power of relationships with my caregivers, though... Let me tell you about them.

My radiation oncologist's gray hair and weathered face tell me he's been at this business for a while. As if he could do it in his sleep, balancing on one leg, with his arms tied behind his back, he runs through everything I can expect regarding treatment and side effects at our first visit. He lights up at the opportunity to share directions via an online map, showing me how to get to the clinic where I'll be irradiated. And when I ask about his family, he tells me about his Thai wife who has grown accustomed to Midwest winters. They've been married for decades and their *kids* are cats.

When I ask why I need radiation if my pathology is clear, Dr. J offers convincing statistics regarding reduced recurrence. What I hear is: It's like irradiating food to reduce germs. It'll increase your shelf life.

I have a trifecta of techs who position me on the table and push the magic buttons for my sixteen sessions. The two biggest challenges are showing up at the correct time and not helping as my caregivers synchronize my tattoos with the machine for targeted zapping. Over the course of three and a half weeks, Henny is my co-pilot, accompanying me on my irregular schedule. She relaxes in the backseat while I enter the clinic and change into a waffle-weave robe. Within minutes, I'm called from the waiting room, positioned, and released to put my street clothes back on. The entire dance usually takes less than ten minutes after which the *fourleg* and I treat ourselves to a romp at the dog park.

Shelly's competence and efficiency is softened with a sprinkle of kindness. Since Halloween is on the holiday horizon, I pick up a few packs of autumn-themed stickers as treats for the techs.

Shelly asks, "Can I stick them on the windows?"

"They are stickers, not clings," I nod. "Whoever has to scrape them off will not be happy."

Before the next day's treatment, I pop into the megamart and find jack-o-lantern window clings that I present to Shelly. For the remainder of my visits, silly pumpkin faces greet me at my entrance and exit.

Young, bright, and warm, Jen is engaged. I can envision her in the wedding dress she tells me she is shopping for. Every time it is her turn to position me on the table, she takes great care to cover my breasts with the towel for modesty. She might not know I notice... but I do. I'm grateful.

One day each week, Robert wears neon pink scrubs. He tells me about his weekend plans and what he's having for dinner. When I give the crew the trilogy of books I wrote, Rob carries them to the protected area on the other side of the glass. The machine clicks and rotates. When Rob comes to release me, he feeds my soul.

"I've already read a chapter! I'm intrigued by the poem titled Accept Differences... pondering the line, 'explore how me is part of us'. Wow!"

It takes about ten treatments before my skin turns pink. For about two weeks after radiation concludes, my skin continues to darken and the burning sensation intensifies. Cracking and peeling are bearable, yet uncomfortable. I liberate myself from a bra, wearing baggy sweaters and sweatshirts. The itch to scratch continues as fall leaves give way to snow flurries, and then one day, I notice this too has passed.

> *I've done it:*
> *Completed*
> *Chemotherapy*
> *Surgery*
> *Radiation*
> *While wearing a can-do attitude accessorized with a*
>   *smile.*
> *Take that cancer.*
> *And thank you for teaching me how to deal with a*
>   *bully.*

Wilbur was now the center of attraction on the farm. . . One day more than a hundred people came to stand at his yard and admire him. Charlotte had written the word RADIANT, and Wilbur really looked radiant as he stood in the golden sunlight. Ever since the spider had befriended him, he had done his best to live up to his reputation. When Charlotte's web said SOME PIG, Wilbur had tried hard to look like some pig. When Charlotte's web said TERRIFIC, Wilbur had tried to look terrific. And now that the web said RADIANT, he did everything possible to make himself glow.

~ E.B. White

36

MAKING A COMEBACK

*I*f I'd had a daughter, I would have named her Grace. And... if I'd had a second daughter, I would have named her Jamie. But it was not in God's plan for me to have a Grace or a Jamie. Instead, I was granted a son. And even though Grant was in the running as a name choice, my husband and I named him Nathaniel, which means *gift from God*.

Tapping away at my keyboard, just days before fellow Americans and I celebrate Thanksgiving, I'm filled with gratitude for the kid's presence in my life. I'll wager he's taught me as much, if not more than I've taught him throughout our lives together. He's likely the greatest invitation to grow that I've ever received. He taught me how to throw a ball and swing a golf club — the syllabus he delivered included practicing patience, culling my temper, and diving deep into my own childhood emotional upheavals.

A space-heater warms my back. I remember the night, dark and cold, just like this one, when Henrietta collided with my chest and called attention to another lesson plan that would change my life. A year has passed since C extended its dance card, and even though I ignored the troublemaker for months, I'm not sorry we eventually worked a two-step together. Cancer has proven itself to be a fine teacher.

I've never shared this with anyone...

When Nathaniel was born, I offered a plea to God. Having been a motherless daughter, I did not want my child to be a motherless son. And so I prayed, "God, please just let me live until he's an adult... and then I will serve in any way you see fit — without question or complaint." My diagnosis came a few months after my boy turned twenty-one.

How's that for *Be careful what you pray for?*

God didn't waste any time. Now that he's seen me through to the other side of c, I feel called to serve cancer patients however the great mystery leads.

Ever so slowly, my hair grows back. In August and September, fresh sprouts felt as soft as kitten's fur. I couldn't stop rubbing my head... and asking others if they'd like to reach out and touch. And even though asking was intimate in a way most Midwesterners are not, almost everybody I asked extended a hand.

An old plastic ruler with faded markings tells me that from

root to tip, my hair has grown an inch and a half from my scalp. My fur grows straight and thick, just as it was before the great fallout. There is one exception, which circles us back to the first paragraph of this love letter... Instead of brunette with blond-ish highlights, my hair is now salt-and-pepper, reminiscent of Jamie (Jamie!) Lee Curtis's short and sassy style.

I recently said to the kid, "I don't think I'm going to go back to coloring my hair."

"Giving up on dyeing?" he asked.

And I swear our brains detected the homophone at the exact same moment because we shared a look and a smile.

"That's right! I'm giving up on dyeing and dying... at least for right now. I'm going to go write that down!"

A mother or a writer never lets good material slip through her fingers.

[Motherhood is] the biggest gamble in the world. It is the glorious life force. It's huge and scary — it's an act of infinite optimism.

~ Gilda Radner

37

YOU GOT THIS

I cannot tell a lie.
 The day is warm.
Flip-flops slap my heels.
Dry, dusty soil settles between my toes and...

Fourleg Henrietta romps and sniffs while I hug the dog park's perimeter.

A red-orange cord, wrapped around a faded fencepost, snags my attention. From a distance I can see the string wears a charm or medallion. I hike up for a closer look. The silver trinket is engraved with three encouraging words — **you got this**. The obvious explanation is that somebody has lost their treasure. A good samaritan must have picked it up and placed it where it could be found.

I want that charm!

My mind starts building a case for me to have it.

Surely a bald, breast-cancer battling woman is meant to have that shiny support?

If you don't take it, somebody else will... a voice I'd rather not claim as my own whispers. It carries on to validate my desire with... *It's not worth anything — made of cheap materials.*

I run my index finger over the engraving and keep walking.

The voice whispers... *That message is there for you.*

And on that, the voice and I are in agreement.

I can own the message without owning the medallion.

More than six months have passed since that summer day.

I'm cured — of my desire to own the trinket... and of breast cancer.

Today, in my snow pants and winter boots, I tramp past the fencepost where *lost-but-not-forgotten* still hangs — cord faded to a pale salmon hue.

Through the seasons, not a soul snagged the physical treasure.

The talisman holds its place — a sign of hope to all who pass and believe the message is sent for them to find.

All I have seen teaches me to trust the Creator for all I have not seen.

~ Ralph Waldo Emerson

38

MATTERS OF THE HEART

P ing!
Never one to ignore the bell, I pick up my cell to see who's sent what.

Soft hues of pink, green, and white wink at me. Peruvian lily petals circle a Gerbera daisy center. The photo and the pings that follow are a gift and greetings from my friend The EarthHeARTist. His creation is titled *Pretty in Pink*.

It's a tribute to... me? And, he's included a blessing that reads:

> May we be brave and face our challenges with the courage and conviction that my friend Gail walked her path with cancer.

I feel humbled to be seen and recognized.

A chance introduction to this friend-of-a-friend took place several months before my diagnosis. He's a former oncology nurse, who currently leads a cancer support group. Does anything ever really happen by chance?

I place my right hand over my heart and feel... nothing. Certain that I'm alive, I stand up and jog in place until I'm panting. Sure enough... Now my palm feels a steady beat through my sweater. I smile at the playfulness that pulled me from my seat.

A year ago, as I lay on a cot covered by a white sheet, a muted technician scanned my heart in a hushed and dimly-lit room at the end of a corridor.

Whoosh, whoosh, whoosh...

Lub-dub, lub-dub, lub-dub...

Tip-tap, tip-tap, tip-tap...

What beautiful sounds flow from a healthy, amplified heart!

Out of respect for my caregiver's quiet demeanor and concentration, I kept my lips zipped and my body still. After weeks of back-to-back medical appointments, I'd set an intention to build a personal connection with every caregiver I met. When the echocardiogram was complete, I asked, "Since I'm lying kind of low these days and looking for inputs to keep my spirits high, I'm wondering if you have any movie recommendations?"

I sensed the question took her by surprise. It took her a couple of heartbeats to answer. *Whoosh, whoosh, whoosh...* "Hmm... sorry. I don't really watch movies."

"How about books, or binge-worthy series?"

Lub-dub, lub-dub, lub-dub... "I do like to read novels —"

I have a huge grin on my face, a giggle in my heart, and a tip-tap in my toes as I recall the genre favored by the heart specialist...

Romance!

———

Wherever you go, go with all your heart.

~ Confucius

39

FOOTPRINTS

*E*xiting the elevator, my soles squeak on the polished floor.

Two months have passed since I last strolled the cancer clinic corridors and I feel joy in my presence here. I have a follow-up visit with my surgeon and a date with the mammography machine to establish a new baseline.

A red plastic shopping bag slung over my fingers holds three cellophane boxes of bakery cookies. I also carry a vase of floral beauty for the petite powerhouse who removed what needed removing. Like a master, she left only a whisper's trace of where she'd trod with her scalpel.

I make eye contact with the receptionist. "Gail Boenning — B-O-E-N-N-I-N-G."

She smiles. "Date of birth?"

I set down the flowers, and the lovely assistant reaches around the plexiglass barricade to fasten a familiar white bracelet around my wrist.

"Are those for Doctor P? They're beautiful. She'll love them!"

"They are," I smile, "and... I've brought cookies to share. What kind do you want for the reception staff? Chocolate chip, fudge brownie, or oatmeal raisin?"

"Fudge brownie!"

"Do I have a minute to deliver a tray to the infusion nurses before my appointment?"

"Sure! Go ahead. If you're called, I'll let the nurse know you'll be right back."

I stride with a spring in my step past the restroom, scale, and private infusion rooms. Sneaking a peek at the #5 bolted to the wall where my favorite heated recliner stands empty, I recall my last infusion...

When the oncologist's nurse walked me over, Lisa guided me to my favored spot — in front of the windows facing the pond where geese, cranes, and herons fish, float, and lounge on the shore. Bay five is where I received my first infusion. Life brought me round full circle so that I could see how much I'd grown.

"Saved you the penthouse," Lisa said with a wink.

Always saddened by endings, tears stung my eyes and the lump in my throat grew. That sunny February day, my team clapped and gifted me an Award of Achievement covered in colorful motivational quotes and well wishes. The framed certificate now hangs on my wall as a reminder to keep going — keep growing.

I exit my reverie when I reach the nurses' station, where I fail to recognize a single saint in scrubs.

"Is Addie here today?" I ask. "Or Katarina? Lisa?"

"No. It's their day off."

My synapses fire. Ahhhh — today is Monday. I was always here on Thursday for my treatments.

"Well, I brought cookies! What flavor do you want? Oatmeal raisin or chocolate chip?"

After making a selection, one of the nurses promises to leave a few cookies for my absent angels. I spell my name again as she jots it down on a yellow sticky.

"I recognize that name." A nurse coming back to the station pauses. "Are you the one who draws all of the pictures?"

I feel flattered, and humbled, and a tiny bit self-conscious. I'm... famous?

"Yup! That's me." Blushing cheeks rise to accentuate my smiling eyes. "Okay... I should go. I have a ten o'clock follow-up with Dr. P."

"Thanks for the treat!"

I float back to the reception area, where a nurse is waiting for me. She leads me through a door to the doctor's office wing, where I step on the scale, light as a feather, feet barely touching the ground — I've come so far.

The people who are crazy enough to think they can change the world are the ones who do.

~ Steve Jobs

40

NOT GOING TO DIE ON THIS HILL

I run a hand through my thick salt-and-pepper pixie. I'm grateful that a square on next week's planner declares HAIRCUT.

Fueled by south-westerly winds, the scalloped hem of my A-line tickles the backs of my thighs.

Is there anything so fine as a seventy-degree spring teaser in early April?

I inhale the bliss of dawn.

A turkey gobbles, and I look downhill to see if I can catch a glimpse. Instead, what catches my eye is a prolific patch of puny weeds, popping through a nearly non-existent layer of mulch.

I sigh.

Young, ambitious, and without awareness of the stubborn nature of weeds, my husband and I built a house on a hill. We ringed it with retaining walls and flowerbeds to solve for un-mowable steepness. Over two decades we've experimented with different plantings including shrub roses, fast growing spruce trees, creeping junipers, and all manner of native wild-flowers. Some varieties thrived for years, while others petered out after only a season or two. What never fails to pop are the dandelions, strong-rooted grasses, and thorn-riffic thistles.

My memory creeps back to last April.

The scene is nearly identical — minus the pixie cut. My bald head is covered with a soft blue bandana. Perhaps instead of a turkey, I am looking for a deer, a rabbit, or a chipmunk freed from hibernation. I see the invasive weeds — an apt metaphor — riding tandem with mutant cells in my breast.

I already have a few chemotherapy infusions under my skin. The weeds needle me, taking root in my mind, blocking the light.

As fortune would have it, a friend of a friend is working toward her coaching certification. She's offering free sessions to accumulate the experience that's required. I'm invited to select a time and directed to come with a problem that's vexing me.

I don't want to talk about cancer or my frustration that after nearly seven years of writing and three self-published books, there are only about twenty people who have read my love letters.

Oh no... no, no, no.

I want her to help me figure out what to do with all of these weeds. Cancer has made it abundantly clear that I do not want to die stooping, bending, digging, plucking, and stabbing at roots on this hill. I'm embedded with a been-there-done-that mindset blossoming into feelings of frustration. You know what they say: What isn't growing is dying.

Going into the video call, I'm aware that in reality, the hill, weeds, and work are nothing more — or less — than an inconvenience. The actual problem is the story I am telling myself, along with my continued reluctance to take action. I stand still — instead of choosing one of the many fields forward.

Josianne and I discuss as much. *Can I change my perception? Can I ask for help? Is it time to move from the hilltop to a prairie? What happens if I just stop plucking and strumming the unwanted?*

Feeling heard by another and having the opportunity to hear myself speak out loud leads me to action. With only slight hesitation, I tap a text to my garden-loving friend, Donna.

> Hi Donna! I'm reaching out because weeds are swallowing my perennials faster than squirrels empty my bird feeder. I can't keep up. If you have time and interest, will you come help?

Of course she'll help.

On our selected date, Mother Nature turns the thermostat up high and the air steamy. I'm certain native Floridians wouldn't work outside in these conditions. I pace the yard before Donna's arrival. Asking for help is a skill I'm working on and now the weather blasts the heat to see what my next play is going to be.

Donna pulls up our drive. We share a hug. She opens her back door to a seat littered with garden tools and implements. Before she can reach in and start unloading, I place a hand on her bare shoulder.

"I'm wondering... it's so hot today. What if we take a tour of the beds, have a glass of tea, and then... instead of pulling weeds... will you come to the garden center with me to pick out annuals for my pots?"

And that's exactly what happens. We share a grand adventure selecting black flowering petunias and purple passion flowers. Together we sweat, laugh, and enjoy the day. Why did I waste even a minute fretting? All is manageable with the right perspective.

Donna returns on a cooler day. After an hour or more of pulling, I play my *I-am-tired-and-fatigued* card to get her to stop. I've no doubt she'd stoop, bend, and meticulously extract undesirable roots until dark. I am blessed in the friendships I have cultivated.

The scalloped hem of my A-line catches a gust.

I'm here now... eyeing that prolific patch of puny weeds.

Grateful to be alive.

Grateful to choose my next move.

Grateful for friendships with deep roots and beautiful blooms.

———

It's not about what someone can do for you; it's who and what the two of you become in each other's presence.

~ Ronald Sharp

41

DIGESTING

April 2023...
    I mound lettuce, peppers, cucumbers, and cherry tomatoes onto half of my dinner plate. A drizzle of French and a sprinkle of bacon dress my greens. I've left room for a small, filled-to-the-brim, steaming ramekin of soup next to the salad.

As I make my way toward a hotel conference-room table, a fellow presenter delivers a thought nudge over my shoulder, "I'm not going to eat until after I've spoken... Don't want to spill on my sweater, smile with spinach in my teeth, or belch like a bullfrog."

I hadn't given such matters any consideration. *Now what?* Do I tuck into my chowder? Or do I allow the heat to dissipate while I wait my turn?

I opt for prudence.

As the keynote speaker tells his story, I watch warm cream congeal around chunks of potato and kernels of corn. The opportunity to share my gratitude with healthcare workers feels momentous. I tell my salivating taste buds and hungry tummy that cold soup is preferable to a gurgling gut.

I'm up!

My short speech is about relational gratitude.

I walk to the podium, remove the microphone from its holder, and begin.

"I want to start with something small." I tug on a corner of the red polka-dotted scarf that's tied around my neck. "All day long we are relating — *relationship-ing* — with our physical environ-ment, the thoughts in our heads, and each other..."

I unknot my neckerchief with my free hand.

"Tonight this square of satin adds color to my outfit..." I hold the scarf up before placing it on my head, "... but last year at this time I had a very different relationship with this synthetic silk."

The audience listens, and several among them engage my gaze as I lay out ingredients for integration ...

- My diagnosis of Triple Negative Breast Cancer in February 2022.
- How self-awareness allows me to choose an attitude of faith, trust, and love.
- How one of the ways this plays out is that I build relationships with my caregivers beyond the transactions of treatment.
- My oncologist and I share a love of ice cream!
- I know where my nurses like to vacation.
- Technicians and receptionists tell me about their families and pets.

Then I delve into the main course of what I want my listeners to hear... three messages that guide my philosophy of forward movement...

The first comes from my oncologist at our initial visit. I asked him, "What causes this disease? Why do I have Triple Negative Breast Cancer?"

His answer tells me he doesn't blame me... and neither should I. "**Dumb luck.**"

The second message comes when a technician inserts a needle into my arm. 'Wow! You are great at your job. I didn't feel a thing."

"**It doesn't have to hurt.**"

The third message is delivered by a nurse who accesses my port for one of my early chemotherapy infusions. We discuss healthy habits relating to diet, exercise, and the people and places that you surround yourself with. As she escorts me back to the waiting room, she shares, "You know... **Some patients leave treatment healthier than they came in.**"

Three things.

I hold up one finger for each.

Dumb luck.

It doesn't have to hurt.
Some patients leave treatment healthier than they
came in.

What I want to leave you with is gratitude — for the relationships you build — with yourself, with the knowledge needed to do your work, with your coworkers, and with the patients who walk through your doors. From a patient who came out of treatment healthier than she came in... Thank you!

I insert the microphone into its holder.

Even though the room is cool, I return to my seat with damp armpits.

I breathe.

The next presenter begins and even though my hunger is now on hiatus, I pick up a spoon and pluck a potato from my bowl. As I eat every morsel from my plate, I wonder how *three things* that set a tone for my cancer journey can become a modus operandi for living beyond cancer.

What happens when...

We set aside blame?

Embrace learning as pain free?

And come through life... better.

When we strive to become better than we are, everything around us becomes better, too.

~ Paulo Coelho

42

ARTISTRY

*E*ighty-eight degrees. A scant six mile-per-hour wind whispers, "Conditions are perfect for your first paddle of the season."

"Can't. Maybe later."

"Why not?"

"Keeping a promise I made to myself."

"Oh... Yourself? She can wait. C'mon!"

"No!"

"Carpe diem!" Wind rustles a few leaves.

"I *am* seizing the day," I say. "Finishing the rough draft of a book about my walk with cancer. Sharing my stories is important to me. Facing one of my biggest fears and coming out on top strengthened my belief in my value."

Wind persists. "If you knew you were going to drop over from a heart attack later today, what would you do? Book or paddle?"

I take a deep inhale.

This is a tough question, a good question, the kind of question we might ask ourselves more often.

"Well... *if I knew*, I'd probably paddle. But! I don't know... We never really know, do we? Life is a game of belief, choice, and action. I believe the odds are in my favor. My heart is full, beating like a champ, so I'm gonna write first, paddle second. If my heart stops beating, I will have died leaving a piece of it behind for others to find."

A chipmunk scurries across deck boards as chickadees flit to and from a feeder full of seed.

As humans, we are all dragons standing between life and death.

We hold the power to decide, creating our lives, one choice at a time.

———

How we spend our days is, of course, how we spend our lives. What we do with this hour, and that one, is what we are doing.

~ Annie Dillard

43

TAKE THE JOURNEY

*I set out
upon the sea
not knowing how
to sail.
At times the unknown
bolsters me;
sometimes
it makes me pale.
Floating without
a place to land
can unnerve
the strongest soul.*

Reaching without
sight of sand
will eventually
take a toll.
Lost betwixt
distant shores...
What options will present?
Are you destined
to search evermore
amid swells that won't relent?
Your biggest challenge
lies inside
What are you made of, lass?
How rough and tumble is your hide?
Can you find
leaves of grass?

I am not afraid of storms, for I am learning how to sail my ship.

~Louisa May Alcott

44

MEET MY THREE MUSES

"Zhen!" Thalia purrs.
   "Jen..." Calliope repeats.
"eh!"
"ah..."
"say!"

"say..."

"kwah!"

"kwah..."

"Jen eh say kwah!" Thalia strings all of the sounds together. She wiggles her fingers at Calliope in a *follow-me* fashion.

"Jen eh say kwah..." Calliope swirls and releases the sounds.

Urania closes her eyes and releases a slow exhale. "French? Oui? Je ne sais quoi?"

"Oui!" Thalia spins and her skirt swirls. "Je ne sais quoi is a quality that cannot be described or named easily. Quite literally — *I do not know what* — an appealing mystery that one dares not examine too closely for fear it will vanish — like reading glasses!"

Fine lines appear around Nia's eyes accentuating her squint. "Very funny."

"Je... ne... sais... quoi," Cal repeats. "Our Typist has found hers?"

"Yes, although it's still a work in progress. There's no doubt that a challenge named cancer nudged our Typist's mysterious evolution forward." Urania's posture straightens. "Storms shift complacency and stagnant patterns of thinking."

"Actually, I don't think it's all that mysterious." Thalia fluffs her curls. "Now that Typist has been confronted with the *BIG-SCARY* that tomorrow might not come, she's plucked up a confidence in herself that she just couldn't grasp before. There's nothing so supple as a woman who has faced her fear — and come out on top."

"That law of life, so cruel and just, [which demands] that one must grow or else pay more for remaining the same."

~Norman Mailer

Calliope, Thalia, and Urania are my muses.

Mysterious as they are, I can tell you my trio of *connectica-tors* are parts of my personality, voices in my head, and companions that guide me through my thinking as I move from one life choice and experience to the next.

Don't we all have voices (errrr... muses) in our heads?

Have you named yours?

Looney-bin-business? Absolutely not! Being aware of and engaging with the voices in our heads as they confront, contradict, and converse with each other is quite sane. Once I started hearing (and actively listening) to my muses, I became a shepherd and stopped being a sheep.

In January 2022, I believed my life was ready to open like a spring crocus. The muses and I started sending out daily love letters to readers of our new blog — 3musesmerge. Together, with me as their Typist, Cal, Tal, and Nia hoped to show others that when you hear your muses, you find your life... or your life finds you.

Little did they know at the time, life was about to pitch a change-up.

The thing that doesn't fit is the thing that's the most interesting: the part that doesn't go according to what you expected.

~Richard Feynman

ABOUT THE AUTHOR

Gail Boenning wanders, wonders, and writes. After facing one of her big *scaries* and coming out on top, she's ready to lasso the world.

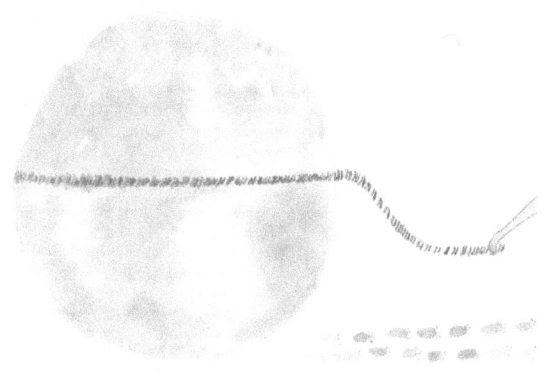

ALSO BY GAIL BOENNING